Awakening of the Third Eye and Chakra Healing

A Guide for Empaths, Mindfulness and Meditations to Develop Psychic Abilities, Clairvoyance and Remote Viewing

3 BOOKS IN 1

Marco Cattaneo GOTAM

Includes:

Intuition

Knowledge and Techniques to Develop Extrasensory Perception

Subtle Body and Chakras

The Energetic Anatomy of the Human Being

Meditation

An introduction to Self-Awareness and Mindfulness in Daily Life

Marco Cattaneo GOTAM

Original title:

Awakening of the Third Eye and Chakra Healing: A Guide for Empaths, Mindfulness and Meditations to Develop Psychic Abilities, Clairvoyance and Remote Viewing

Published by: GOTAM CAMDA MEDIA

Editing and proofreading: Claudia Marchione

Cover image and illustrations: iStockPhoto, licensed to Marco Cattaneo.

First edition: August 2022

ISBN Paper Edition: 9781915718006

Intuition

Knowledge and Techniques to Develop Extrasensory Perception

Marco Cattaneo GOTAM

Claudia Marchione CAMDA

Dedicated to you as a reader and me as a writer, because in our journey of growth we have chosen to devote time to the most important person in our lives - ourselves - and, for once, we will look inside rather than looking outside.

Marco Cattaneo GOTAM

Foreword (Marco Cattaneo)

When Claudia, who has been participating in my meditation groups for a few years, asked me for some time to talk about intuition, I couldn't help but record our conversation and get this book out of it.

In most cases, when talking about extrasensory perceptions, people think this ability belongs to two types of individuals: charlatans or *mediums* born with special sensitivity. This book was created to debunk the myth that intuition is reserved for those chosen few, and to teach anyone who wishes to develop this wonderful ability the key tools to achieve it.

I can't say I was born *clairvoyant*. Until the age of twenty-four, I was always very rational and scientific in my approach to life, and perhaps for this very reason, I had to learn through hard work to take my higher perceptions into account, developing this talent day by day.

After more than a decade of practice, I had the opportunity to summarize my experience into this small book, with the aim of helping those who are curious, and who feel their perceptions emerge, to know and use them consciously.

My intention is not to create a *complete* work on the subject, but to provide examples and suggestions that can allow you to better *tune into a particular dimension of your being and open your mind.*

Claudia, who joined me in this journey with her questions, was already familiar with the phenomena you will read about. However, she also knows that it is easy to achieve an extraordinary evolution by acquiring information on these subjects.

While words shape your mind and perception, if you choose to focus your attention on this ability you can completely change the game of life.

By reading questions and answers about intuition, you will feel something's changing inside yourself.

Since I am not only a Reiki Master and meditation teacher, but I have also been working with hypnosis and unconscious communication for a long time, *let my words soak in* and you will enjoy interesting benefits.

In order to ensure that the following suggestions and stories remain effective, I have chosen to preserve their original structure and the colloquial nature of their style. Accept the fact that some linguistic forms may not strictly follow grammatical rules and that there may be some 'poetic license'. This is also part of the game.

Contrary to common belief, the human mind learns much more easily in a non-sequential way. Give up the attempt to follow the logical thread of subjects and let this new knowledge take shape, fragment by fragment.

Do not expect a scientific essay; it is not possible to fully understand intuition in a rational way, while it is necessary to experience it concretely in one's own life in order to benefit from it. I have decided to keep this text short in order to make it more usable by anyone.

This handbook should be read once, from beginning to end, so that the information contained in each chapter can soak in and build the foundation for what follows. You can re-read it at a later stage to get ideas, insights and exercises for the development of extrasensory perceptions.

Read slowly, because to get to the end without enjoying the journey would be a real shame.

Whenever you encounter the Eye of Ra symbol (e.g. at the end of this chapter), take a break for a few seconds and let the acquired information flow into your mind. If you don't fully understand the meaning of a sentence, *just keep reading*, because you will find an explanation a little further on.

Since Claudia has been a participant in my workshops for years and she also graduated in Foreign Languages, she has edited and reviewed this book herself, with the help of her dear friend Holly Renaut.

Enjoy the read, but above all, *start opening up your Mind.*

Non-Introduction (Claudia Marchione)

A few years ago, I approached meditation for personal needs, and after a hesitant beginning, I continued tenaciously (and probably will continue forever), because as I meditated I saw myself change. And as I changed, the world changed with me.

I could go on forever and talk about who I was, where I wanted to go and who I've become... but the truth is that each person has their own story, their own motivations and their own thoughts. *And yours are the ones that matter*.

On the other hand, I was simply a curious girl who was never satisfied with the explanations given by adults, because her world had always seemed more varied and colorful than what they wanted her to think.

For some reason, at certain times in life, you feel the urge to do something different, to find answers to the questions that have been buzzing in your head for a long time, at any cost. Just like *Alice in Wonderland* who follows the White Rabbit down the rabbit hole, you know you have to go all the way to discover the wonder that awaits you.

I have always been an apparently extroverted person, but with very thick armor and little confidence in other people. I have always had 'unusual' perceptions, but for a long time I didn't even wonder where they came from. Until at some point in my life, I started to have unexplained health problems and realized that the only way to deal with the world outside was to find out who I really was *inside*.

I wasn't even thirty years old when I first asked Marco, my Reiki and Meditation master, to spend some time talking about intuition and new perceptions that, through my journey, I was experiencing more and more frequently.

To be honest, I didn't expect talking about intuition to mean looking through the keyhole of such a fascinating universe. I found not only an explanation for the feelings that occasionally emerged within me, but also a new way of seeing the world that I couldn't imagine before.

Marco teaches disciplines that help you to realize who you are and how the world around you *really* works. He is eager for knowledge, and he is always looking for new tools. He knows how to explain complex topics in simple words, and he is able to lead journeys in and out of oneself.

I have chosen to ask him my questions because I believe that truth springs from an insatiable curiosity and that the best way to teach is to learn new things every day.

Through my interviews – between 2014 and 2015 – I tried to express the connection between reason and feeling; between the world we perceive and reality; between the masks we show and what we really are.

By doing this, I learned the importance of putting your thoughts on hold and making room for what you feel deep inside yourself.

I hope this book is just the beginning of *your* exciting journey of discovery.

Intuition can transform your life for the better: *seeing is believing*.

Please note: The whole book is developed in the form of an interview. For ease of reading, the questions and comments of the narrator were written in SMALL CAPITAL.

Chapter 1

«HI MARCO, THANK YOU FOR AGREEING TO ANSWER SOME QUESTIONS ABOUT INTUITION. I WOULD LIKE TO EXAMINE SOME ASPECTS OF THIS FASCINATING MATTER IN DEPTH.»

«Talking about intuition (and explaining what is usually confidential information through this book) really amuses me, and gives me the opportunity to share a long journey that has brought much wonder into my life.»

«I'D START WITH THIS QUESTION: WHAT IS INTUITION EXACTLY?»

«Intuition is the ability through which we can draw on information that lies in a different dimension of time and space than the *current* one, it is the ability that allows us to perceive beyond the five senses and the chance to access to the past or the future in a non-linear way.

Intuition is the complementary element to rationality, the perfect complement to logical thinking.»

«WHAT DO YOU MEAN WHEN YOU SAY "PERCEIVE BEYOND THE FIVE SENSES"?»

«We are used to living, perceiving reality, relating to other people and collecting information through sight, hearing, smell, taste, touch, and then processing this information within us.

Intuition is the so-called sixth sense, "a channel" that many people use, even if they don't know exactly what it is and how it works.

We often ignore some *strange* perceptions that come to our mind, we refuse a concrete explanation for their presence. When this information corresponds to real events, we label what happened as "coincidence".

By consciously training to use this ability, you can understand its nature and learn how to use it to your advantage.

We could use, as synonyms of intuition, the words "clairvoyance" and "clairaudience". We can find these terms in ancient esoteric schools, in several philosophies or religions; their meaning is deep-rooted in the very nature of any human being.

This is an important aspect, which I'd like to emphasize; when we talk about intuition, clairvoyance or extrasensory perceptions, we refer to a part of nature within every human being, to a possibility available to each and every one.

While some people are more used to *living* this possibility, to letting this ability free, other people are simply unaware of its existence (because of the education they have received or their level of self-awareness).»

«ARE YOU SAYING INTUITION IS WITHIN EVERYONE'S REACH? OR PERHAPS THERE ARE TALENTED PEOPLE, WHO WERE BORN WITH THIS "GIFT" ...

IS IT REALLY SOMETHING YOU CAN DEVELOP?

THE EXPRESSION "THIS IS MY PERSONALITY, I AM WHAT I AM" COMES TO MIND, VERY OFTEN USED TO JUSTIFY THE PRESENCE OR ABSENCE OF A CERTAIN TRAIT OF THEIR BEING.

PEOPLE WHO DON'T RECOGNIZE THIS ABILITY WITHIN THEMSELVES, HARDLY ACCEPT THEY CAN DEVELOP IT.»

«It is not easy to distinguish what characterizes us from birth from what we learn later; what has always belonged to our nature from what we *become growing up* and receiving an education.

As we know, our personality and our character develop from the very first years of life and are influenced by the significant emotional experiences that happen to us.

By carefully observing children aged three or four, we notice "peculiar" behaviors related to the perception of reality around them; how many of them talk to imaginary friends, for example?

If we look at a teenager or a young adult instead, certain behaviors have been basically lost.

The education we receive (more properly, we should call it *conditioning*) allows us to set some traits of our being free over others. In the last decade, epigenetics has explained very well how our own genes can be "activated" or "deactivated" by environmental and emotional conditions (therefore, it doesn't really matter whether a genetic characteristic is present or not, the important thing is whether it is activated or remains unexpressed).

In addition to aptitudes and genetic expressions, our brain increases those areas we use the most and our mind follows those "patterns" and cognitive processes to which we are most accustomed.

It is scientifically evident that the human being is *a continuous becoming*. We still know little about our nature and we generally express only a part of it.

Intuition is connected to the creative part of the brain, rather than the logical and rational part.

Because of everything that I have just explained, some find themselves living this ability more easily, others instead have learned to limit and ignore it (and therefore need to unveil it).

Intuition is certainly something that is part of our nature, it is a superior "ability" of our mind, that is connected to the right hemisphere of the brain.

Recognizing the so-called dominance of the hemispheres is important to understand why some people are apparently more intuitive than others.

Generally speaking, we can say that the left hemisphere of the brain is "the engineer"; besides being specialized in linguistic processing, it is more competent in the sequential process and in the perception-management of events that follow one another over time (such as the logical connection of thoughts). In other words, the engineer-brain is more qualified in the analytical perception of reality.

The right hemisphere, on the other hand, is the "intuitive poet", more specialized in visual processing and perception of images, their spatial organization and emotional interpretation. To put it briefly, the poet-brain is responsible for the global and overall perception of stimuli.

We could compare intuition to the so-called "lateral thinking" promulgated by psychologist Edward de Bono; while our analytical mind is able to develop "linear" reasoning, the intuitive mind can put together and manage information in a completely different way, *beyond the limits* of cause and effect, space and time.»

Intuition is an ability that belongs to every human being, some of us just need to relearn how to use it.

Chapter 2

IN MY PERSONAL JOURNEY TOWARDS SELF-AWARENESS THROUGH MEDITATION, I HAD THE OPPORTUNITY MANY TIMES TO EXPERIENCE PERCEPTIONS OUT OF THE ORDINARY, BECAUSE WHEN YOU CLOSE YOUR EYES AND JUST LISTEN (LIMITING THE SENSORY PERCEPTION OF THE WORLD AROUND YOU), SUDDENLY SOMETHING BIGGER CAN HAPPEN.

BY EXPERIENCING INTUITION, WE BEGIN TO OPEN OUR MINDS AND HEARTS TO WHAT WE CONSIDERED IMPOSSIBLE BEFORE.

I'D LIKE TO ASK MARCO SOME MORE INFORMATION ABOUT CLAIRVOYANCE BECAUSE, I DON'T KNOW ABOUT YOU, BUT I AM VERY CURIOUS ABOUT THIS KIND OF PHENOMENA.

«YOU'VE TALKED ABOUT CLAIRVOYANCE AS A SYNONYM FOR INTUITION. SO... ARE THEY THE SAME THING? WHAT ARE CLAIRVOYANCE AND CLAIRAUDIENCE EXACTLY?»

«Clairvoyance is the visual component of intuition, the perception of images within our minds. I'm not talking about what we perceive with our physical eyes, the visual channel that collects information from the outside, but rather about a "mental" perception.

While intuition is generally the ability to access information beyond the limits of space and time, clairvoyance is the inner visual reception of that information.

Ancient philosophies also speak of clairaudience, that is, the ability to listen in one's head, through the auditory channel, to information intuitively perceived.

There are also clairsentient people who live intuition through the sense of touch, smell or taste. In fact, we can "kinesthetically" perceive some intuitive information, simply having the feeling of knowing.

All these types of perception are similarly extrasensory and, in some cases, generally defined with the term *clairvoyance*, so it can become a synonym for intuition.

When you really went through a certain event or were present in a situation, if you think about it, you can remember the feeling and know *how* you experienced it.

We can recognize an intuition because of a similar feeling; we know that something "is true", but we do not know *how* that information came to us.

A subtle channel, a privileged path in relation to the senses that connect us to the outside world, carries information directly to the consciousness.»

DESPITE THE FACT I'VE ALWAYS BEEN FASCINATED BY THIS TOPIC, I COULDN'T HELP BUT DEAL WITH A WIDESPREAD SKEPTICISM ON THE SUBJECT.

I THOUGHT OF PLAYING "THE DEVIL'S ADVOCATE" AND PUT MARCO TO THE TEST, IN ORDER TO UNDERSTAND WHAT HE THINKS ABOUT IT.

«TO BE COMPLETELY HONEST, WHEN SOMEONE TALKS ABOUT CLAIRVOYANCE IT ALWAYS REMINDS ME OF FORTUNE TELLERS IN FAIRS, AND HOW THEY "SEE" YOUR FUTURE... AND, ALTHOUGH I HAVE PERSONALLY EXPERIENCED THE INTUITIVE PROCESS DURING MY MEDITATION PRACTICE OVER THE YEARS, THIS SUBJECT STILL LOOKS SOMEWHAT MYSTERIOUS TO ME.»

«I totally understand you», SAYS MARCO, SMILING.

«Often I think back to the person I was fifteen years ago.

Just to help you understand what I'm talking about: I ran a leading IT company in Italy, I defined its processes, I spent my days relating to software developers, engineers, and I myself had an extremely scientific, rational and rigid approach to life.

My right hemisphere was still very, very much asleep when I was living *that life.*

I am still very efficient at using the rational mind and I understand how absurd a subject like this can sound, at first.

However, skeptical people are divided into two groups; the obtuse and the smart skeptics. Obtuse skeptics, when they come into contact with new information, dismiss it out of hand because of narrow-mindedness. Smart skeptics, on the other hand, recognize that it's something new, and decide to suspend their judgement to gather information and understand if that innovation can give a new meaning to life.

The path beyond the boundaries of what we already know, after all, often leads to marvel and amazement!

I myself support healthy, smart skepticism, not unconditional faith. Do not blindly believe that intuition exists. Give yourself the opportunity to *actually* experiment and verify whether you can gather information beyond the five physical senses, although science, while using this ability to its own advantage, hasn't fully explained it yet.

Is there any curious or particular aspect about intuition that "tickles" or intrigues you?

It's time to go deeper, to better understand how all this can *feel real*.

It's been a long time since I was living *that life*.

I can't say that I've changed my mind overnight or that I've gone through some magical passage of "spiritual awakening".

I simply learned to make room for the other half of my brain to expand and opened my mind.

Precisely because I have been so rational and rigid, I have always tried to *understand*, and ironically this helped me a lot. I have studied the human being and the mind for over a decade, specialized in neuroscience, studied medical and anatomical texts, examined the mechanisms that guide our perception, learned Neuro-linguistic programming and Hypnosis in most of their forms and applications (including therapeutic aspects), I know the impact of communication on human psychology and I have approached the topic of intuition from the most skeptical point of view possible.

And, finally, I had to *give up*.

I know how, *at first*, intuition can seem absurd and inexplicable, and I also understand that a word such as clairvoyance calls somewhat peculiar characters to mind (a middle ground between entertainers, charlatans and gurus).

I admit that it is not immediately easy to understand the nature of this "miracle" of our essence.

It's absolutely normal. When we try to understand, to explain and "rationalize" intuition, we are using that part of the brain that has nothing to do with intuition itself.

There is a moment when you realize that *you have to decide to give up the need to understand and start feeling the intuition.*

If it's any consolation, just as the rational mind struggles with the creative-intuitive mind, the creative-intuitive mind also can't really understand the rational one », MARCO LETS OUT A BELLY LAUGH.

«When you choose to lower the volume of your critical mind, calm down those thinking processes we use to judge and understand, and begin to use the other part of your mind, you start having a different comprehension and perception of that privileged channel of contact with reality.»

Chapter 3

«HOW WOULD YOU EXPLAIN THE DIFFERENCE BETWEEN UNDERSTANDING THROUGH ANALYSIS AND PERCEIVING WITH SENSATIONS?»

«When you read a book, you leaf through its pages, point your eyes at the words and pronounce them in your head.

Basically, our eyes catch the visual stimulus, photograph the words in front of them and project this information onto the visual cortex (a sort of screen that is in the back of our brain).

Then, as most of us learn to read aloud at school, the inner dialogue produces the sound of those words before our eyes. We mentally repeat what we read with our eyes, one word after another.

Just realize this process right now, while you're reading.

Yet... how do we know the meaning of the words we are reading?

I know it may sound like a strange question, but think about it: how do you know that a specific word means a specific thing?

Our mind is truly fascinating and hides many secrets. We tend to use it more in *some specific ways*, but we need to be aware of a number of processes that happen within it and the *lateral* potential that characterizes it.

The reading process takes place in several different stages. I'm suggesting this analogy because it gets easier to understand; we have to collect visual information, and listen again to the voice in our head, before we understand.

The actual understanding of what we read happens through the sensation we *feel* within us.

If I read a written word, for example "HOUSE", first I see the word "HOUSE", then I repeat the word "HOUSE" in my head, and my mind generates a sensation that allows me to know its meaning.

What you feel within you is your actual meaning of reality.

When we have an intuition, we feel that we know something, even if we completely lack the visual or auditory process that allowed us to collect that information from the outside world.

We feel something without knowing *how* or *where* it came from.

When you start putting this sensitivity into play in relationships and life, you can begin to understand it a lot more.

We generally use our five senses to gather information because our consciousness is more in touch with this dimension of reality (and this is how we were educated). But there are other channels that convey a parallel flow of reality to our mind.

Although our common way of thinking doesn't include an ability such as clairvoyance, labelling it as "charlatan stuff", we all experience events and situations where some information *inexplicably* comes to our mind.

Naturally, our rational mind tries to understand everything.

In ancient times, when people experienced a situation they couldn't explain, they easily attributed it to a deity or to magic. Today, we tend to do the same thing and, even more simply, we call it a "coincidence".

I was born in 1983 and today I am thirty-three years old. I grew up in a society permeated by the scientific method, by a rational vision of the humankind and, also thanks to this, I was able to link scientific research on human anatomy to the ability of intuition.

Unfortunately, we don't yet have a complete demonstration of what intuition is, even though plenty of research and experimentation has been done on the subject.

Much is said about this ability because, in complete honesty, it is really difficult to deny the existence of a non-visible dimension in our nature.

For centuries, medical science has considered human beings to be biological machines, almost robots, composed of systems interacting with each other. Yet each of us feels that we have a soul, that we are something more than a machine (even if we can't explain it scientifically).

Although I received a religious education since the early years of my life and always came to terms with spirituality, rationality unquestionably prevailed up to a certain age.

When I started developing awareness of myself and life in general, becoming aware of what is happening before my eyes every day (and of many unexplained events from a rational point of view), then I began to doubt my certainties.

Science itself knows so little about our brains, and almost nothing about what we call the "mind" and the mechanisms that drive it.

Mind and brain are two very distinct things; the brain is the organ that is in our skull, while the mind is something indefinite. We usually feel it in our head and at the same time we know it is connected to our consciousness and soul.

Only when I discovered there were more methods beyond the rational one to explain certain events and correlations, did I realize that some peculiar situations – that were already happening – began to acquire a clear meaning.

I began my journey to discover intuition, and the training of this perceptual ability has given me endless satisfaction.

Besides everything I've just said, I'm also convinced that some fortune tellers use their imagination, rather than intuition. This may be useful in order to recognize clearly what's intuition and what's *charlatanism.*»

Exercise 1: Recognizing the structure of thoughts, memories and intuitions

In relation to any knowledge you know you have (for example, *"the sky is blue"*), ask yourself the question *"How do I know that?"* and put your answer into words out loud.

- When the answer contains events from the past, experiences or sensory perceptions, what you are analyzing is not intuitive information. You can also recognize a memory, or an experience, by the emotion that the thought brings with it; the memory is in fact a connection between a mental image and the sensation-emotion felt when the event took place.
- When you can't answer by explaining *how* you know what you know, and you are simply aware of the thought that goes through your mind, you are analyzing intuitive information. You may also notice that intuitive information is not associated with emotions (although it may happen that you "react" emotionally to the intuition received).

Chapter 4

«You said you did a rather "rigid" and very rational job, that you grew up in an environment with a strong scientific culture.

Was there a moment, when something happened that made you "open the door" to a new dimension?

Did you start developing this ability of intuition "out of nowhere" or did you approach a specific practice? How did it happen?»

«It's difficult to identify a precise moment when I realized I had intuition. I think it is simply part of our (and therefore also mine) nature since we were born. I just became aware of what it was. I decided to believe in it and use it consciously.

At the unconscious level, we constantly receive information from the intuitive channel and use it every day in our lives. But precisely because we do it *automatically*, we don't know *how* this can happen.

The first step is not to start developing intuition, but to realize that we already have it, to realize what happens in our minds at all times.

One of the main obstacles to intuition is what we commonly call "stress", as well as a pace of life that is too frantic compared to our natural one.

As we *slow down our actions and thoughts*, we can begin to notice this ability more easily. From there, we have to follow the path of training and practice.

I realized I had this ability when I began to look around me at unusual situations that occurred too frequently, and I said to myself, "If this thing is happening today... tomorrow... tomorrow again, maybe there's a pattern here and what I have always considered a coincidence, could have a different meaning".

Twelve years ago, I got interested in meditation, hypnosis and states of consciousness, and I began to gather valuable fragments and explanations to unravel the knot.

The practice of meditation has led me through my *Intuition Training*; that ability has grown, because just like so many aspects of our character (unconscious programming that triggers our emotions), it can be trained and improved greatly.

Many exercises and practices imply intuition and make it *easier* to use.»

Chapter 5

«DO YOU HAVE ANY EXAMPLES? WHICH PRACTICES CAN BE USED TO TRAIN INTUITION?»

«In my experience, meditation works like a laser, by focusing vital energy on a fundamental point for intuition (the so-called "third eye" or sixth chakra) so that we can develop a new level of *vision*.

On the other hand, the constant practice of Reiki in my path forced me to use intuition, to lower the volume of my thoughts, of the rational mind (which works and creates noise within us most of the time) and to let something deeper emerge.

Reiki is a discipline that allows you to work on physical, mental, emotional and psychic health, channeling vital energy to a receiving person through the heart and hands.

Practicing Reiki means bringing one's hands closer to various parts of another person's body, providing more vital energy to nourish them.

There is no "mental requirement", no kind of visualization or rational process, just *stay in touch and let it flow*.

No "doing" is required, just *be open* and *let it happen.*

Starting to practice Reiki, more than during meditation, I found myself with a calmer mind; practicing Reiki means to stay in deep contact with the other person, to keep listening. It is almost as if every part of you becomes an antenna, which can receive what is around it.

While I keep my attention on kinesthetic information (i.e. present in the body) and I practice Reiki, my mind *receives* images, sounds and sensations from "other dimensions".

My teachers told me, "Keep your attention on tactile sensations, this is the important aspect" and in doing so, I found myself receiving images, sensations or voices, which somehow allowed me to know places I normally had no access to.

I practice Reiki with my eyes closed, my hands in contact with a person I often don't know and I've never seen before; I don't talk to them (because no preliminary interview is required), but as I stay in that position, I receive information about their story and their life. Sometimes as clear as a movie.

In this form of meditation and presence in the *here and now,* I found myself noticing new information in my mind and asking myself, "Where does it come from?"

The trick was to recognize that some information was different from other information. Sometimes I perceived it coming from the mind », Marco POINTS AT HIS RIGHT TEMPLE.

«Sometimes from a higher channel» AND HE POINTS AT AN AREA BEHIND AND ABOVE HIS HEAD.

«In fact, it is one thing to think (i.e. to construct images in your mind, following what eyes, ears, touch, taste and sense of smell *carry* within us), and a different thing to perceive what appears through the connection with a *wider field.*

It's very important to *see the difference.* Intuitive perceptions, unlike memories and thoughts, do not generate emotions, but only the certainty of knowing. If a thought comes from past experience, it has been associated with the emotion lived during the experience itself. Intuitive perception, instead, appears within us "for the first time" and doesn't belong to our history.

During a Reiki treatment I have my eyes closed (I'm not using my physical eyes), the scenes of life are not in front of me, however they come inside my head.

As time went by, I began to value this new information received and to verify it.

So, I started asking people I was treating, "Are you married?" if I felt that they were.

Sometimes I was much more specific, "Are you married and you have three children, one of whom doesn't live with you?" or "Do you have a son named Michael?" ... and when I received affirmative answers, I tried to pretend nothing happened (in order to avoid the mutual embarrassment of not being able to explain how I could have that information).

Eventually, as I continued to verify this information in the real world, I got more confident in my intuitive ability and I realized that perceptions were becoming more and more specific and frequent.»

«YOU TALKED ABOUT MEDITATION AND I AM VERY FAMILIAR WITH THIS SUBJECT, BECAUSE I'VE BEEN PRACTICING MEDITATION FOR SOME YEARS NOW. YET MOST PEOPLE HAVE BARELY HEARD OF IT. COULD YOU EXPLAIN IT IN MORE DETAIL?»

«On the door of the Delphic Oracle temple was the inscription "Know Thyself", and this is the key to a full, rich and satisfying life.

What is meditation?

Meditation, in all its forms, is an extraordinary tool for transforming your life, breaking down useless ego structures built on your true being and, ultimately, developing intuition.

It is a state of consciousness that brings us into contact with all that is authentic in us and in the reality around us, with the only moment that really exists: the present moment.

46

According to studies by Stanford University's Center for Research and Education on Altruism and Compassion (directed by Dr. Emma Seppala), through meditation we can improve the functioning of the immune system and reduce physical pain, increase happiness and positive emotions (reducing depressive symptoms, anxiety and stress), improve social relations, emotional intelligence, self-control, attention and memory. Loneliness also decreases, while work performance, creativity, the ability to think outside the box and wisdom increase.

In some cases, the practice of meditation is only a vain attempt to reach such a state of consciousness... because this requires time and patience, but at the same time it is an extraordinary path of discovery. Sometimes, instead, meditation just happens!

We can meditate by focusing conscious attention on breathing or on a "fixed" and specific thought, on the repetition of a mantra or a prayer, on a simple movement or on our sensations in the body.

We can only know meditation through practice. For this reason, when I welcome new people into my groups, I invite them to practice immediately, before any explanation.

Meditation brings us into contact with our vital energy and raises its vibration. What am I talking about?

Chinese people already referred to it as *Chi* thousands of years ago, Japanese people call it *Ki*, Indian people call it *Prana*. In Europe, Hermes Trismegistus referred to it as *Telesmae* and, almost simultaneously, Hippocrates described the *Vis Medicatrix Naturae*, Paracelsus called it *Munia*, Kepler *Facultas Furmatrix*, Goethe *Gestaltung*, and Galvani simply *Vital Energy*, Mesmer called it *Animal Magnetism*, von Reichenbach *Odic Force* and, as we approach the present day, also Einstein, Freud, Jung, Steiner, Reich... all talked about energy as a substance that constitutes life.

Everything is energy, we are energy.

The quality of our energy determines the quality of our life; the higher it is, the closer we get to the transcendent nature of reality, to our invisible essence and intuition.

Practicing meditation together with other people is key (individual energy adds up to the group energy), but often people don't have enough time, and practice groups are scarce in many cities.

For those who'd like to live the experience of meditation, I have created a Free online training program, as well as a number of Guided Meditations.

To begin with, all you need to enter this fascinating world is some essential information and a desire to know yourself in depth.

I'll take this opportunity to further explore the subject of Reiki.

Reiki is a method to rebalance the vital energy of our system, by positively influencing body, mind and emotions. It is a path of spiritual evolution that involves an open heart and a focus on its energy.

Only by receiving a Reiki treatment from a master or a qualified (and experienced!) practitioner can you really know its nature.

Again, don't get persuaded by what people say, just *let yourself feel.*»

Exercise 2: Basic meditation "The Power of Breathing"

This guided meditation helps you to stay present by focusing your attention on breathing and allows you to restore a more natural and conscious state.

The relaxing and regenerating effect gives clarity of mind and fulfillment.

It can be repeated several times a day and a practice series of twenty-one consecutive days is suggested.

PREPARATION:

- Sit in the Yoga "easy pose", sitting cross-legged in a natural way (alternatively, remain comfortably seated on a chair);
- Keep your back naturally straight;
- Bring the tips of your thumb and index finger together, the back of your hands on the knees, and keep the other three fingers open upwards;
- Keep your arms and shoulders relaxed.

EXECUTION:

Step 1 (3 minutes):

- Breathe smoothly and naturally, breathe slowly and deeply;

- The abdominal area expands during IN-halation, the abdominal area moves back in toward the spinal column during EX-halation;

Step 2 (4 minutes):

- Breathe smoothly and naturally, breathe slowly and deeply;
- During IN-halation first expand your abdomen, then your chest, filling "the space" up to the collarbones;
- During EX-halation first empty the upper body (collarbones and chest) and then the abdomen;

Step 3 (4 minutes):

- Stay in contact with the feeling of the air coming in and out of your body, while visualizing a light moving with your breath in your mind and listening to its "sound";
- Visualize in your mind IN-halation as gaining new energy;
- Visualize in your mind EX-halation as letting go of all tensions in your body and mind;
- Exhale and take your mind back to the outside world, return to a normal position.

Chapter 6

«BACK TO INTUITION. THE MORE WE GO ON, THE MORE THIS THING CAN SEEM ABSURD AND UNCONVENTIONAL TO THE EARS OF PEOPLE WHO DON'T KNOW MUCH ABOUT IT...»

«Irrational, I would say», MARCO SMILES.

«... IRRATIONAL, EXACTLY! WHILE RESPECTING THE PRIVACY OF PEOPLE INVOLVED, CAN YOU TELL US SOME STORIES OR SHARE ANY EXPERIENCES ABOUT INTUITION?»

«Yes, I have many actually. Countless.

Some of these experiences are related to my activity as a Reiki master and practitioner, meditation group teacher or coach, while others are personal experiences of my daily life.

I am an entrepreneur, I run some businesses and therefore I deal with organizing purely logistical and practical aspects for these companies. Obviously, I also have a social life in which I interact with other people, and at some point, even out there, intuition begun to take shape.

For me, these situations are absolutely real, because when I treat a person I don't know and I can think of the name of their dog or their children... I can't dismiss these perceptions as a "coincidence".

During a treatment, a few years ago, I had the *feeling* of a rectangular ticket. I was treating someone I'd never seen before, and I asked, "Does a long, narrow ticket mean anything to you?" and he asked me, "What do you mean?" so I said, "I saw a rectangular ticket, like an airplane ticket," and in that moment the person told me "Maybe it's because I work at the Fiumicino airport and I handle a lot of tickets all day long."

Some information comes in a very precise way, some is less clear and needs to be linked to the individual experience of the individual before it can be understood.

During some treatments, more recently, I happened to perceive serious problems in specific parts of the body. In very rare cases, I suggest people have a medical check-up as a result of a sensation I received. In a specific case with a woman, doctors actually found she had a tumor in her uterus (fortunately it was successfully treated at an early stage).

Less frequently, I have auditory perceptions, but sometimes it happens that words or phrases help me to focus my attention where the treatment is needed most. While treating a fellow Reiki Master, I identified a specific problem with his prostate (during the meditation the word "prostate" resonated in my mind) and, shortly after, he confirmed to me that he had already received a critical diagnosis about this.

In some cases, the perception is similar to a movie I see with my eyes closed; a long series of scenes shows me the history of that person and leads to the understanding of their psycho-physical condition.

One of the biggest challenges is not to judge what arrives and to provide intuitive information as accurately as possible. Practice teaches you how to do it with excellent results.

Often intuition is triggered by the emotional baggage people bring with them, and it can be perceived in the energy field around their body. As an example, I move my hands closer to the liver, I perceive the residual anger of a past trauma and, being open to receive, I get the image of a controlling father who intensely yelled at his son and his sense of helplessness as he couldn't react.

A very young girl I treated was carrying a great "sense of control". When I moved my hands closer to her abdomen, I had a *flashback* of her mother educating her by holding emotions back and controlling tones of voice and gestures.

Sometimes people are surprised that I know details of their lives, but in most cases, they are too busy thinking about what I just said to worry about how I know it.

I can go on and on with many stories... and I have to admit that this inside track towards different realities still fascinates me deeply, even after such a long time.

Thankfully, it's not always bad news that comes through intuition! During a recent seminar, three different people (including myself) perceived the figure of one of the participants accompanied by a newborn baby. Later we discovered that she had been trying to have a baby with her partner for over two years. Six weeks later she discovered, this time through the classic pregnancy test, that she was finally pregnant.

Sometimes intuition helps me too, and not just the people I meet.

In everyday life, since the sensory inputs we receive from the outside world are much stronger, it is easier to observe that we know something without noticing the mental images (it's not quite important *how* intuitive perception reaches us, we can learn to recognize it through different channels!).

I remember one morning when I felt particularly centered and inspired. I sensed a kind of circle around my forehead; the strong feeling that my vital energy had reached a good level.

I was waiting in line to top up my Roman public transport pass. I had the strong feeling that the employee in front of me would mistype the cost of the pass and a few moments later, when my turn arrived, that is exactly what happened. The lady on the other side of the desk typed an incorrect number during the transaction.

Interesting intuitive events can take place through dreams. Even though I finished high school fourteen years ago, I happened to dream of my Italian teacher (while living in a city that is five hundred kilometers away from my hometown) and meet her ten days later, for the first time in a very long time, walking along the promenade near my old high school.

When these situations occur, it is worth stopping and thinking about them. How extraordinary our nature can be?

On more than one occasion, although I had an appointment scheduled, I had the clear feeling that I didn't have to go to the chosen place (even if I didn't know exactly why). In these cases, unless I check by phone, I find myself waiting in vain for the person I have to meet who forgets about the meeting or is very late.

Besides recognizing an intuition, you must also *learn to listen to it*.

At first it is not easy, because logic contradicts higher perception, but this is precisely the greatest challenge: rebalancing the rational mind and the intuitive mind.

Another classic example (which I'm sure has happened at least once to everyone): for more than a year I hadn't heard from my friend Cristina, and while I was working on my computer, the image of her face came to my mind. A couple of hours later, Cristina called me to ask me for advice.

As I have studied the mind and unconscious strategies, I can assure you that it is not possible to find an explanation for this "magic" without transcending the boundaries of mind and body... looking *beyond*.

I need to emphasize that these phenomena happen outside the domain of reason. I assure you that living these experiences personally is even more amazing than reading about them in a book!

A few years ago, I was introduced to a woman at a work lunch and I immediately had the feeling of which emotional knot she should untangle at that time of her life. After I introduced myself and shook hands with her, I immediately asked, "Do you have any children?" She went pale and her eyes were glistening, because she had been trying for a long time without success.

In everyday life, it is much easier to let intuition happen than to "strive to receive information". However, you must have practiced first!

Before I start a Reiki treatment, a group meditation or an individual session, I focus my attention on opening the intuitive channel. This is more than enough, because every morning I meditate to be receptive and present.

Statistics can't explain why everyone has experienced thinking of a person they haven't contacted in months and receiving a call from them shortly after. For this reason, it's necessary to bring attention to *wherever these kinds of situations occur and to perceive them with different eyes.*»

«YOU WERE SUGGESTING THAT WE "LET GO", THAT WE LEARN HOW TO KEEP OUR THOUGHTS QUIET THROUGH MEDITATION. WHAT IS THE CONNECTION BETWEEN INTUITION AND THOUGHT? IS IT NORMAL FOR SOMEONE, EVEN WHILE MEDITATING, TO HAVE THOUGHTS AND MISTAKE THEM FOR INTUITIONS OR VICE VERSA? WHAT IS THE DIFFERENCE BETWEEN THINKING AND KNOWING INTUITIVELY? HOW DO YOU RECOGNIZE WHETHER A THOUGHT HAS AN INTUITIVE ORIGIN OR IS THE RESULT OF REASONING?»

« I'll answer your question right away.

Anyone can feel the existence of a space within the mind, a theater where images, sounds and voices crowd together during their lives.

Only a part of what is staged in that theater is intuition.

By studying Neuro-linguistic programming, for example, we can better understand which mechanisms control our (conscious and unconscious) thinking, and most importantly, we can modify them permanently.

Why do I get angry about a statement? What makes me feel safe or insecure in a certain situation? How do I make decisions exactly? What motivates me or holds me back? What mechanisms trigger self-destructive or toxic behavior? Why can't we avoid certain types of people? How do we complicate personal or work relationships so much?

The explanation is always in a neuro-associative conditioning to which we respond automatically (even if we don't like to admit it), habits that are repeated outside our level of *awareness*.

Have you ever heard of Pavlov's dog?

Psychologist Ivan Pavlov would ring a bell every time a dog started to salivate when food was presented. After a few repetitions, even without food, the animal reacted by salivating to the sound of the bell.

The same stimulus-response association works perfectly on human beings; when parents and educators prepare us for life, they create strategies of emotional action and reaction within us.

A specific tone of voice, gesture or facial expression of the people around us can instantly bring us back into a certain emotional state and make us react accordingly.

Over time, we refer to these habits as "personality" and "way of being", but these behaviors have nothing to do with intuition. They are connected, instead, to the unconscious and reactive mind.

In addition to (present, past and future) memories, to that voice inside our head we use to speak to ourselves, there are some *different* images, sounds and sensations. They don't originate from a process of conditioned thinking, instead they *flow* to us through a connection to a higher realm.

Science has almost managed to understand it (although I don't think it will ever be a "globally" accepted truth) and I am happy to explain it.

If you use a scientific approach to understand the world, you soon discover that a scientific theory is considered "true" only until someone can prove otherwise.

Until recently, science said that it was the Sun that revolved around the Earth! In history we find many examples of scientific truths suddenly collapsing under the weight of new discoveries, the so-called "paradigm shifts".

Many doctors and scientists participated in my seminars over the years, so I had the opportunity to discuss important issues with them. Having to deal with scientists, you realize that within the same paradigm and at the same time, many different opinions coexist (all apparently valid and verified even if radically contradictory to each other).

It is the very history of human beings and their different points of view.

Over the centuries, science has contradicted itself countless times; a truth in the eyes of Newtonian physics can be disproved by string physics (although these two paradigms are both considered valid).

Not to mention psychology. Most scientists don't consider it a science, even though it is widely recognized in common thinking.

Yet we continue to rely on the scientific method because we are constantly looking for "certainty" and "control". It is the need for safety that leads us to believe what *seems most certain.*

Newtonian physics (which is still studied today in high schools) is a paradigm completely revolutionized by Einstein's relativism, later evolved into string physics and M-theory.

This long digression is just to say that much of the information that comes from "official science" is interesting as it can help us understand the world, but it is not necessarily "true".

Do we really need a scientific proof to believe and make a difference?

I really like the example suggested by Lissa Rankin in her book "Mind over medicine" (I absolutely recommend reading it); when a method is used to cure a person's illness and this saves their life, it can't be considered a scientific truth at all, yet... a human being is still alive instead of being dead, and it should mean something!

Now, it's normal and right that someone verifies the repeatability of processes, cures and procedures according to the scientific method, however, we must learn how to develop our personal *sense of truth.*

Intuition, just like medicine, can really save a life. That's why I am really glad I can talk about it frankly.

By using intuitive information, we can avoid self-sabotage, unconscious choices and quite a lot of pain, set ourselves free from the boundaries of our cognitive mind and misleading sensory perception.

Our eyes only see within a limited range of light frequencies (for example, we can't see the infrared or ultraviolet range), our ears only sense certain sound frequencies (we can't hear ultrasounds), yet we know there is a reality beyond these limits... but how can we access this reality if our senses don't allow us to do so?

Each eye has a so-called "blind spot" (the area of the retina where the optic nerve leaves the eye), but our brain generalizes the image it receives, by mixing data coming from both eyes, and prevent us from seeing a "hole" in that spot. Our nose is technically inside our own field of vision, and yet we don't see it consciously (because this information is deleted by our brain).

Do you see where I am going here?

Bulls see the world in black and white, eagles see more colors than any human being can imagine (because their eyes have more photoreceptors than ours), humans see colors that eagles can't perceive.

Who sees colors as they really are: bulls, eagles or humans?

Everyone… or perhaps no one, you would answer.

Optics, in fact, explains that color is not an "intrinsic feature" of an object, but it is the result of how light interacts with the object itself and with those who perceive it.

Technically, the grass *is* not green, we *see* it green (because it absorbs all the light waves *except* the green one).

Moreover, we have to add cognitive limits to the physiological limits of our perceptive system. Our mind generalizes, distorts and deletes information received from the outside world, filtering the sensory perception through our opinions and through what we consider to be true.

We have the car keys in front of us, but in the rush of leaving the house we can't see them.

When we choose a specific model of car to buy, shortly after we see that specific model in every corner of the city. Reality didn't change, our focus did!

In general, our conscious mind can perceive a limited number of stimuli, and our focus is influenced by what's important to us and by our previous choices.

People perceive reality through their personal point of view, filtering events through their beliefs and their own perceptual ability.

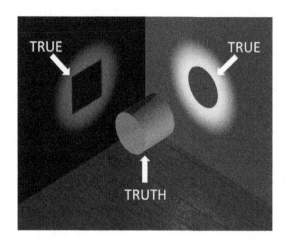

Something is missing.

Through intuition we go beyond the boundaries of our rationality and access a much wider field of perception.

This alternative channel, which brings information to our mind, allows us to enter a realm that has different rules than our reactive thinking.

The conscious mind can manage a handful of information, compared to the unconscious mind that can manage millions of pieces of information at any given moment.

This distinction is crucial; we have to identify a number of processes that happen while we are paying attention to them, and other processes - most of them, as Freud describes with the metaphor of the submerged iceberg - that are far from our consciousness.

We must learn to become aware of what is happening beyond our common threshold of awareness.

Just as our unconscious mind carries on the emotional and motor processes (staying in balance, driving the car or performing complex athletic gestures), processing information through the rules we learned in childhood, everything that comes from the intuitive channel is also managed according to rules already internalized.

Observation of the mind lets you learn to identify thoughts that seemed to blend with intuitions at first.

Thinking is something very close to intuition, in terms of time and space, because they both happen in our minds. They are two extremely different abilities, even if they can feed each other (an intuition can be useful for rational reasoning, just as reasoning can be a gateway to new intuitions sometimes).

We can see that, while it is our ability to consciously generate thought, we can only *let intuition happen.*»

Chapter 7

«So, it would seem that you need some confidence in relying on intuition... in trusting what you feel. Is there any kind of underlying "awareness"?»

«In my experience, trust in intuition was born from study and introspection, while it grew through practice and feedback received.

Ancient philosophies and religions have always talked about it, but the mind of the individual can only begin to see when he believes (exactly the opposite of *what the masses do*; expecting to see in order to believe).

Over the years, I researched and integrated practices into my life that could produce intuitive thoughts.

I kept working with people through intuition and trying to get feedback on any information that might arrive.

The more you use intuition; the more you get excited about intuition in your life, the more you get to enjoy what you do and *how* you do it. When you live using intuition, you rediscover an extraordinary power; the power of managing your reality, doing it with fewer mistakes, gambling less on decisions, and acquiring the ability to "look through walls".

It reminds me of the cartoon of Dr. Quantum, the episode in which he talked about multiple dimensions of reality (you can find the video in the *Intuition Training Arena*).

There is a little round creature, a little circle with eyes and mouth, that lives in a world with just two dimensions: it can only move forward and backward, to its right and to its left.

Its senses perceive only two dimensions, and in its world the word "above" is very scary (because no one knows exactly what it means!).

One day, a human being - living in a three-dimensional world - touches it in the middle of its belly and the little creature feels a strange sensation. The human being, who is mistaken for a deity, tells it, "I am above you", and the animated circle gets scared and begins to tremble, "You don't say that word! It scares me!"

The human being, suddenly, takes the creature between two fingers and raises him, making it live the third dimension, and it is speechless and goes, "oooohhhhh!".

And this is how it works for us too; we are used to thinking in three dimensions, with time flowing linearly from the past, through the present and towards the future, and any alternative *seems* absurd and could frighten us.

Only through the sixth sense can we escape from these illusory limits and regain the ability to move freely in *new dimensions*.

The point is that our mind doesn't think much about what it does, about its own mechanisms. Only when you start to use it to look at yourself can something interesting happen»

«I'M A LITTLE BEWILDERED THAT YOU'RE TALKING ABOUT IT LIKE IT'S SOMETHING VERY NATURAL AND SIMPLE.

IT MAY LOOK NORMAL TO YOU, BUT HOW DOES AN ORDINARY PERSON APPROACH INTUITION AND DEVELOP A SENSE OF AWARENESS? ARE THERE ANY PRACTICES OR TRICKS?»

«Yes. There are very fascinating initiatory journeys to develop intuition.

I consider it a natural ability, also because I have friends and collaborators who, just like me, use intuition very well. These people are re-educating their minds to work to the fullest.

The main enemy of intuition is an unnatural lifestyle, characterized by a high amount of stress. Because if you feel that your mind is working too much, that it's overwhelmed, and emotions such as dread and fear are very present in your life, you won't be able to access your higher abilities very easily.

If there's a warning light on your car dashboard, you simply focus on the message it carries.

The first step in releasing intuition is to let your natural rhythm of life *come out*, to stand out from the crowd.

The feeling of not being able to escape certain "obligations" imposed from the outside is pure illusion, a mix of fear and habit of abdicating our decision-making power. When we make a choice and make room for what is important to us, the world around us changes its shape accordingly and finds ways to provide us with the resources to achieve what we want. Unconditionally.

We fear the head of the office won't grant us the holidays we need, we are scared of making our voice heard, making mistakes... or being judged by other people.

Without warning and without money, five years ago, I quit my (very well paid) office job overnight and I chose to build a life tailored to my needs.

After deciding to do so and training my subconscious to succeed, I was informed that the company I was managing had been sold, and that although I was guaranteed a year's salary, the new owner would have it managed by someone he trusted.

I was then invited to stay home, enjoying my usual salary... and my new freedom.

The following week I "accidentally" received €30,000 in block grants, with which I started my first independent activity.

When you really feel you want to do something, you don't need safety nets: *you are the safety net!* You have the power to create any reality you want through conscious thoughts, words, decisions and actions.

You need courage (from the Latin words "cor" and "agere", the ability to act with the Heart) and intuition.

Fulfilling one's "will" is the only real obligation of every human being.

Have you ever tried any of those music tracks to synchronize the cerebral hemispheres?

(I suggest you try Holosync by Centerpointe Research Institute.)

When our rational and intuitive minds work in sync, we automatically enter into meditation, in a state where space and time have a completely different taste.

In that state of increased presence, our concerns and the buzz of the world around us just stop. Issues work themselves out (or perhaps we realize those problems never existed in the first place).

When these two dimensions of the mind align and become coherent, intuition arises spontaneously. Meditating on the third eye for one hour a day is almost useless if you are living someone else's life, if you are nervous or constantly worried. Intuitive information will come, but you won't be able to notice it.

If you were running late for work, checking Facebook and listening to music all at the same time, and an oracle on the side of the road whispered, "Don't go to the office today, a disaster will happen." You wouldn't be able to hear that guiding voice!

Being aware of this is the first step. Then you need to have the courage to listen to it.

First of all, you have to find your core and your natural flow, quiet external impositions and give importance to yourself. Contact with the present moment and mastery of your own emotions are necessary.

Meditation is certainly a very powerful practice to unfold our *vision*, especially meditation focused on the chakras.

In the Hindu culture - and in most of the ancient cultures of the world - the term Chakra is used (or *energy centers* of a similar nature).

The term Chakra comes from Sanskrit and means wheel. Chakras are energy centers in the body, with the purpose of exchanging information on various levels of consciousness.

The concept of Chakra is closely linked to that of our personality and our way of being; we can consider these energy wheels as portals through which we filter and bring to consciousness parts of information belonging to less tangible levels of being.

Each chakra encodes the data under its own specific light, allowing you to observe situations in a different way each time, as through the various facets of a crystal. Although closely related to our physical body, chakras are not immediately perceptible through the five senses, because they are in the so-called subtle body.

Each chakra is connected to a part of the body, to certain emotions, and to certain aspects of life.

A chakra is also a bridge that connects any human being to the universe in which they live; each chakra corresponds to a color, a musical note, a planet and specific foods.»

THE 7 CHAKRAS ACCORDING TO HINDU CULTURE

1st Chakra: perineum region, connected to the excretory system, related to "grounding in reality", instincts and survival;

2nd Chakra: genital region, connected to the reproductive system, related to emotions (including pleasure) and sexuality;

3rd Chakra: solar plexus (navel), connected to the digestive track, related to ego, character and personality;

4th Chakra: center of the sternum (heart), connected to the cardiovascular system, related to unconditional love and passion for life;

5th Chakra: throat, connected to the respiratory system, related to the most authentic self-expression and communication;

6th Chakra: center between the eyebrows (third eye), connected to the central nervous system, related to thinking, creativity, intuition and extrasensory perception;

7th Chakra: above the top of the head, connected to the peripheral nervous system, related to spirituality and oneness with everything that exists.

«The sixth chakra is linked to thought, vision, perception and creativity, placed between the eyebrows, it's the center to which the ability of intuition is connected. It corresponds to the so-called the *third eye*, the pineal gland.

By its nature, a chakra can be more or less flowing, more or less harmonic. A disharmonious sixth chakra corresponds to hyper-rationality, difficulties in fully perceiving reality, intellectual arrogance, dogmatism, rejection of intuition.

Focused meditation on this center can allow to rebalance the different nuances of mind and perception, and to increase extrasensory vision.»

Exercise 3: Basic meditation "Chakras and Breath"

This basic meditation guides you in focusing your attention and breath on each one of the 7 Chakras.

This practice increases vital state and facilitates the balance of the seven dimensions of being.

Daily listening is suggested, for a practice series of at least twenty-one consecutive days.

PREPARATION:

- Sit in the Yoga "easy pose", sitting cross-legged in a natural way (alternatively, remain comfortably seated on a chair);
- Keep your back naturally straight;
- Bring the tips of your thumb and index finger together, the back of your hands on the knees, and keep the other three fingers open upwards;
- Keep your arms and shoulders relaxed.

EXECUTION:

- Breathe smoothly and naturally, breathe slowly, deeply and consciously (staying in contact with the feeling of the air coming in and out of your body);
- Breathe consciously on the 1st Chakra

(perineum region), feeling the air coming in and out of that point towards the ground and visualizing in your mind a white light coming in and out of the body in that same point;

- Breathe consciously on the 2nd Chakra (genital region), feeling the air coming in and out of that point and visualizing in your mind a white light coming in and out of the body in that same point;
- Breathe consciously on the 3rd Chakra (navel), feeling the air coming in and out of that point and visualizing in your mind a white light coming in and out of the body in that same point;
- Breathe consciously on the 4th Chakra (center of the chest), feeling the air coming in and out of that point and visualizing in your mind a white light coming in and out of the body in that same point;
- Breathe consciously on the 5th Chakra (epiglottis), feeling the air coming in and out of that point and visualizing in your mind a white light coming in and out of the body in that same point;
- Breathe consciously on the 6th Chakra (between the eyebrows), feeling the air coming in and out of that point and visualizing in your mind a white light coming in and out of the body in that same point;
- Breathe consciously on the 7th Chakra (above the top of the head), feeling the air coming in

and out of that point upwards and visualizing in your mind a white light coming in and out of the body in that same point;

- Breathe consciously on all 7 Chakras simultaneously, visualizing in your mind a white light coming in and out all seven points;
- Breathe at a natural pace and stay focused on how you are feeling in this moment.

«While studying the nature of the pineal gland, some interesting aspects were observed. The name "pineal gland" comes from its shape, as it looks like a small pine cone. Inside this gland is a liquid that tends to calcify from four years of age onwards and decalcifies during R.E.M. sleep or meditation.

Inside this liquid are photosensitive cells (like those of the eyes!), which therefore seem capable of perceiving different light vibrations.

Between the two cerebral hemispheres, in short, there is a gland which resembles an eye and sees forms of light that our eyes cannot see.

By focusing attention on this area, just behind the forehead, it is possible to decalcify the liquid of the pineal gland and *keep the intuitive vision open*.

This practice requires time (different from one person to another) and patience.

Meditation modifies the body, directs the vital energy towards this ability, while the conscious attention to the intuitive information coming to our mind allows us to re-educate the cognitive aspect.

It is important to accept that intuitive information has nothing to do with dimensions of space and time as we usually understand them.

We need to learn how to practice the sixth sense, as well as any other ability. You can contract and stretch a muscle to strengthen it, repeat an athletic gesture thousands of times to carry out a sport and, similarly, *you have to practice to reactivate the vision* that was left atrophied for years, so that it works at its best.

Meditation is a very simple and extremely powerful tool, both to become aware of our mind (and how it works) and to calm the internal rhythm and focus the vital energy where it can reactivate the intuitive perception.

Today we know that meditation radically modifies the physics of the brain and the size of some of its areas.

For over ten years I have been meditating regularly on the third eye, where the pineal gland is, and the more I do this, the more I have extraordinary visions and perceptions.»

Exercise 4: Advanced meditation on the Third Eye

This advanced meditation supports your intuition and extrasensory perception development by working on the 6th Chakra (third eye).

It should be combined and alternated with basic meditations (Exercises 2 and 3).

PREPARATION:

- Sit in the Yoga "easy pose", sitting cross-legged in a natural way (alternatively, remain comfortably seated on a chair);
- Keep your back naturally straight;
- Bring the tips of your thumb and index finger together, the back of your hands on the knees, and keep the other three fingers open upwards;
- Keep your arms and shoulders relaxed.

EXECUTION:

Step 1:

- Breathe smoothly and naturally, breathe slowly and deeply;
- During IN-halation first expand your abdomen, then your chest, filling "the space" up to the collarbones;
- During EX-halation first empty the upper body

(collarbones and chest) and then the abdomen;

Step 2:

- Take 5 deep breaths focusing on the 1st Chakra (perineum region);
- Take 5 deep breaths focusing on the 2nd Chakra (genital region);
- Take 5 deep breaths focusing on the 3rd Chakra (navel);
- Take 5 deep breaths focusing on the 4th Chakra (center of the chest);
- Take 5 deep breaths focusing on the 5th Chakra (epiglottis);
- Take 5 deep breaths focusing on the 6th Chakra (between the eyebrows);
- Take 5 deep breaths focusing on the 7th Chakra (above the top of the head).

Step 3:

- Check your position (shoulders and arms relaxed, straight back);
- Relax your forehead, cheekbones, and the muscles behind your ears;
- Bring your attention and breath to the third eye, repeating three times a "triangular breathing" (inhaling, holding your breath and exhaling performed for identical times);
- Deeply inhale and exhale making the sound "*thoh*" (protracted) focusing on the third eye

(repeat 6 times);

- Breathe at a natural pace for a few moments;
- Deeply inhale and exhale making the sound *"may"* (protracted) focusing on the third eye (repeat 6 times);
- Breathe at a natural pace for a few moments;
- Use the state of meditation thus created to obtain specific information (by asking a clear question) and listen to the inner feelings that emerge or face a particular situation in your day;
- Exhale and take your mind back to the outside world, return to a normal position.

«In which moments of our life can we receive intuitive information from our mind? Only in a waking state?»

«Intuition happens even more easily when our state of consciousness is expanded. In the so-called "non-ordinary states of consciousness" (so called although they are actually much more common than you think).

Dreams are an excellent gateway to extrasensory and unconscious communication. Easily, during sleep, we can receive or rework intuitive information that has previously reached our mind. We just have to learn to "look at" it without judgment and, ironically, without trying to interpret anything.

Hypnotic trance and the meditative state itself greatly facilitate the channeling of intuitive information.

In daily life an *agonistic trance* can help us a lot to integrate intuition into what we are doing; what is commonly called "flow state" (or "the zone" in sports) is a state of optimal functioning of the mind, in which our consciousness is in simultaneous contact with the outside (through the senses) and with the inside (kinesthetic, intuitive sensations and thoughts) in a constant exchange of information.

Living in a flow state means choosing and setting a goal, abandoning yourself to the flow of things, letting the *how* be the result of deeper and higher forces than the conscious will alone.

It is the difference between swimming in the sea against the current or being carried by the right current that leads to the shore; in the second case no effort is needed, nor are too many strokes.

The flow state, if you think about it, happens naturally every time we are particularly competent in carrying out a certain action. We have defined an objective or a goal and we know we can trust ourselves.

We can feel at a different level (and put our intuition into play) while we get a massage, while we drive a car in contact with the environment around us, while we work creatively as a craftsman... during a sport or work performance that is important to us... it is essential, in any case, that the mind is "present" to our gestures (and not "somewhere else").»

«WE'VE TALKED ABOUT CLAIRVOYANCE AND INTUITION. I WONDER IF THE PERCEPTION OF THE AURA IS RELATED TO THESE ABILITIES.»

«Yes, perception of the aura is connected to clairvoyance and *clairsentience*.

By developing the ability to perceive beyond the five senses, you can begin to feel or see the energy field of humans, objects and places more easily.

Perception of the aura is one of the most fascinating aspects of the invisible world; it gives you the feeling of having X-rays and being able to see through people's emotional life (as well as history). The aura, in fact, contains traces of the experience of each of us, of the emotions that we live more frequently and intensely, and therefore a map of our past and future.

Again, this is not an ability that appears overnight, it requires time and gradual development.

There are some exercises to bring you closer to perception of the aura, but even in this case, it is basically a matter of developing a lifestyle and dedication to the process of amplifying your perceptions – rather than a simple sensory training.

As with intuitive perceptions of past and future, this ability must be "earned". I don't mean that someone or something gives us this power, but that we have to learn and lower the level of judgment in order to access this information domain.

The subject is very broad and I prefer to talk about it another time.»

Chapter 8

«RETURNING TO PRECOGNITION, OUT OF CURIOSITY: LISTENING TO YOUR STORIES, I WOULD SAY THAT IT'S EASIER TO PERCEIVE "NEGATIVE EMOTIONS AND SITUATIONS". IS THIS REALLY THE CASE?»

«In my experience, it is more frequent to gather information related to traumatic events, but that doesn't mean you can't perceive funny events or joyful experiences as well!

I believe that in the therapeutic context it's more frequent to come into contact with traumas and burdens simply because both players are focused on solving the problem and the key is always in an emotional *imprinting* from the past.

Sometimes, luckily, you are able to gather information about happy moments or particular perceptions, such as "open-mindedness". For example, for some people I've felt that having travelled for a long time had *opened* their minds. I have tested this intuition at least three times with different people and I was actually right, all of them had travelled for many years, in contact with different continents and cultures. Another fascinating sensation is the feeling of "integrity" and "inner strength"; some people carry with them a "core" of wisdom and greatness of spirit.

In any case, if you think about it, an event is never either "positive" or "negative" in itself; it is the mind that observes it, according to its own schemes and the conditioning received, and judges it in one way or the other.

Although it may not be easy to accept, there is no objective perception of reality that can reach our brain through the five senses, nor is there a universally valid point of view on what is good or bad.

Just think of some actions that the law of one country punishes harshly as crimes, while the law of another country considers them absolutely legitimate and normal.
Polygamy is legal for ninety percent of the world's cultures, but absurd for ours. Using opium and marijuana is a tradition practiced by people of all ages in South America, but we strictly condemn it. Beatings and mutilations are often perpetrated on many minorities in many countries...

The narrowness of personal judgement leads us to the paradox of perceiving a behavior as negative and, at the same time, punishing it through the same act (imposing the death penalty on a murderer, for example).

We are generally inclined to consider our personal point of view as the most appropriate, because this is what reasoning and "our gut" tell us.

My intention is not to change anyone's mind about what is good or bad, precisely because whatever the judgment expressed, it comes from the limits of the mind.

From an intuitive point of view, every action performed or suffered has a precise purpose. To be able to understand it, it's necessary to consider this action from a wider perspective than the individual one.

Anyone who has grown up in a Christian-Catholic culture clearly perceives the sense of good and evil that the religious institution has transmitted to us. However, from an intuitive point of view, what the mind can judge as being negative is always a reason for significant growth for the individual, and it is essentially something they need.

Intuitive perception allows us to overcome the limits of mental judgment and to understand events that have already happened in a much wider context.»

«NOW A SLIGHTLY MORE "TECHNICAL" QUESTION: HOW CAN SOMEONE HAVE AN INTUITION ABOUT SOMETHING THAT HAS YET TO HAPPEN OR PERCEIVE SOMETHING THAT HAPPENED A LONG TIME AGO?»

«However difficult this may be for our minds, in order to understand this phenomenon, we must be open to extraordinary scenarios. Many scientists who have studied quantum physics explain that time may not *work* at all as we perceive it.

The superstring theory describes the reality in which we live, at infinitely small levels, composed of eleven dimensions. Much more than the four we normally perceive.

Some people have postulated the existence of more than one dimension of time.

Just imagine you are looking at any object in detail, getting closer to the deep structure of its material, to the point of discovering that it's not made up of three dimensions at all, but seven (computers are able to draw multidimensional models that, as absurd as they may seem, give the idea of a reality with more than three dimensions).

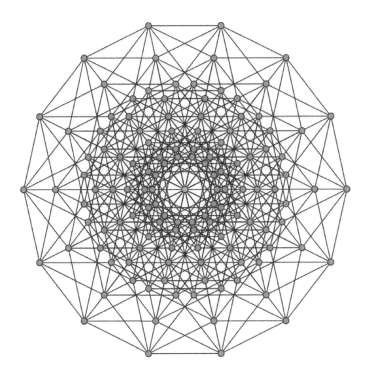

Seven-dimensional hypercube (shown through a
two-dimensional image)

Source: Wikipedia

The mind is short-circuiting, isn't it? And this is just the
beginning.

We are used to mentally representing time as a linear
dimension. In this model there is a past, a present and
a future somehow connected to each other, and our
mind perceives that the passing of time starts from
the past, *through* the present and *towards* the future.

Depending on your perception of time, some things that did make *sense* may no longer do so.

If you accept a linear perception of time without discussing it, then thinking you can access future information in advance has no explanation, because the future is yet to *happen*.

But if you assume for a moment that present, past and future could be set *side by side* (as if the time *line* changed direction and was placed horizontally) and that consciousness could move horizontally from one to the other, free to access everything that is happening in the future *at this very moment*, then you can begin to feel its fascination.

Unfortunately, many people talk about quantum physics without knowing anything about it...

A movie that conveys mostly precise information on some theories of quantum physics is *"What the bleep do we know?"*, a sort of documentary that talks about how our perception of reality is limited and filtered.

Well, I can't say exactly what time is and how it works, because even my rational mind perceives time like all of you, but still...

Time *in a way* exists because we measure it.

Think about it. If there were no clocks hanging on our walls or watches on our wrists, time wouldn't exist in the same way. If no one had invented the clock, our life would be different and our relationship with time completely new, because the moment we measure time, we make it real. The moment we measure time, then time begins to exist. Not only with timepieces, but also in our own minds; time exists because we compare two different moments (*yesterday* with *today* or *today* with *tomorrow*, for instance).

But when we live in a meditative state and *we are in the eternal present*, linear time no longer exists and neither do the limits that prevent us from moving to another moment.»

«IF PAST, PRESENT AND FUTURE WERE ACTUALLY HAPPENING AT THE SAME TIME, WE COULD "ACCESS THE FUTURE" BECAUSE IT WOULDN'T BE DIFFERENT FROM THE PRESENT, INDEED. SO CAN YOU TELL ME IF IT'S GOING TO RAIN TOMORROW?» I ASK JOKINGLY.

«Sorry, I can't predict the future. Simply because there is not *one* future!

Let me conclude my explanation to make you better understand how absurd this quantum world is.

Aside from the unreal "direction" of time, the game becomes even more fun when you start to consider a second dimension of time.

Try to imagine that, in addition to the dimension already described, time develops into a "vertical" series of different planes, arranged one above the other.

If this were the case, there would not only be a present, a past and a future side by side, but *infinite presents*, *infinite pasts* and *infinite futures* that form a matrix on which our consciousness can move.

Quantum physics describes the observer as the true "creator" of reality (through the historical and now famous double-split experiment, for which a detailed explanation can be found in the *Intuition Training Arena*).

In a nutshell, we could say that in this experiment an electron can assume infinite different behaviors at the same time. However, if one observes its behavior, it is defined and specific and no longer "multiple". It wasn't possible to explain how this is possible (i.e. why this happens), although this is actually what happens.

This "inexplicable oddity" of subatomic reality has not yet been experimentally verified in a macroscopic dimension, however it has marked the beginning of a probabilistic vision of reality (as opposed to the previous deterministic one) and provides us with a possible explanation for otherwise uncanny phenomena.

The concept is represented in the metaphor of Erwin Schrödinger's cat. According to the scientist's thought experiment, a cat in a box together with a "trap" is both alive and dead, until an observation takes place. In that moment, the observer would *choose* which reality to live in.

Without an observer, therefore, the cat would be simultaneously alive and dead, because both realities exist until a conscience *decides to tune in* to one of the planes of existence, to one of the possible realities. That reality, in that moment, would become their "real present".

All of this may seem unlikely to our senses.

Truth be told, even scientists who made these same discoveries find it hard to accept their *actual* value.

As I said, I don't know how time actually works or what time actually is. The point is that if we begin to admit the possibility that things may work differently from what we experience, then intuition may have a different meaning, intuition may have an explanation in a certain sense... in the sixth sense!», MARCO LAUGHS.

«Technically, I cannot predict *the* future, but *a* future. The one on which consciousness is tuned at that moment. But that future can change, because it is just one of the possible realities.

Imagine someone walking in a meadow and there is a tree along their trajectory; if they kept walking in that same direction, they would bump into that tree. But if they changed direction (even by only a few degrees) they would completely avoid it.

This is one of the extraordinary abilities we possess: to choose and change.

The very fact of predicting the current future can be a good reason to consider a change, even if it's not always as simple as it seems in the movies.

In some cases, changing reality requires an important emotional awareness, the healing of an open wound, or simply reprogramming one of our beliefs.

In most cases, I avoid talking and giving importance to a *vision of the future*, unless that vision is about myself and I want to change the plane of reality in which my consciousness is *currently* tuned.

Informing a person about a vision of their future can trigger an unconscious pain chain where fear and worry may prevail. It's the same situation you see in medical science when you make an unfortunate diagnosis; based on *how* a certain piece of news is told, a person can feel condemned to a given end, although actually, right from that moment, the future can be changed.

The predicted future is nothing more than one of the infinite possibilities that could become real; a somewhat more likely possibility than any other because of human beings' struggle to change themselves – and with that, their journey.

Similarly, when I perceive an event from the past, I don't necessarily see what "it was", but what the person (or myself) experienced and especially *how* they felt it.

It often happens that a person is carrying the emotion of past physical or psychological violence. In some cases, an event is, indeed, attributable to abuse (what we might commonly consider violence), but in other situations an ordinary event was simply perceived as a violation.

When working with intuition, you must learn to distinguish with attention and deference the vision-sensation received and the interpretation that your mind can give of it. It is equally important to learn how to properly share the information obtained, so that it conveys the creative potential they have in their own hands to the person concerned. The future, just like the past, can be transformed through consciousness.

In order to learn how to effectively communicate your intuitions, I suggest describing what has come to your mind by reducing the qualifiers to a minimum (which often derive from your own judgment) and, above all, avoiding "free associations". For instance, referring to a rectangular ticket you have perceived (as in the example in chapter 6) is quite different from talking about a ticket for a football match!

As you open up to new ideas about the world and reality, some abilities begin to emerge.

Now it's interesting and fascinating, isn't it?

It is, in fact, the great curiosity these themes have always aroused in me that has pushed me beyond my limits and allowed me to transcend the "boxes" that were my prison.

When our minds are firmly convinced of something, we are basically "imprisoned" in that reality.

The movie *The Truman Show* is a good example of this; as long as we live within a built scenario and cannot transcend its boundaries, *go beyond*, rather than pass through its walls, we can't see we are within a closed perimeter. While the moment we manage to transcend that perimeter is the moment we begin to discover a new reality.

I am still amazed and fascinated by intuition, after many years, precisely because the rational mind cannot fully understand it.»

Chapter 9

«WHAT CAN YOU TELL ME ABOUT COLD READING? WHAT IS THE RELATIONSHIP BETWEEN INTUITION AND COLD READING?»

«They are very different things, essentially two opposite things.

Cold reading is the ability to gather information by observing another person, a kind of reading of one's body language and features.

Cold reading may seem like magic, but it has a very specific foundation.

Talking about magic, when we see a card trick, our first reaction is "Wow! That's amazing!", but if you search for the series "Magic Finally Revealed" on the internet you can find many magician's tricks revealed, and from that moment on, when you see a card trick you will have X-rays; you will know how to recognize the secret.

Many magicians are actually illusionists who use their handiness to create the illusion of magic.

Cold reading may look extraordinary, but it is just deductive intelligence.

The same goes for mentalism; it is some kind of specific and hypnotic communication which can condition people's behavior in advance, in order to put on a show and amaze people by giving the impression they can predict it. If you really know NLP, it's easy to see the mechanisms behind mentalism.

Often in TV shows we see so-called magicians predicting the future, while using simple cold reading or mentalism combined with artfully vague language (which allows them to make a statement that doesn't deny reality and, actually, feels like it has a specific meaning).

I know these "techniques" very well. They can be useful, interesting to study and even therapeutic, but they have nothing to do with real intuition.

I think there is nothing wrong in combining different "techniques", you just have to recognize the source of the information you gather.

In one scenario you can use your senses to notice aspects few people can see, in the other one you are drawing from a higher source.

Through cold reading it wouldn't be possible to know the proper name of a person, while through intuition I just have to place my hands near that person, keep my inner voice quiet and listen to what comes to me.»

«IT LOOKS LIKE INTUITION BRINGS A BIG RESPONSIBILITY WITH IT, TOWARDS OURSELVES AND THE PEOPLE AROUND US. IT'S LIKE

«Yes, I also feel a great responsibility that comes from using intuition, and at the same time, thinking about the last ten years of study and practice of this ability, I also realize that it increases as my awareness develops, and it is inversely proportionate to the judgment on other people and events.

Only when I suspend judgment, lower the volume of thoughts and relate authentically with a person, can intuition find its place, and intuitive information remains pure when it reaches my mind.

When the analytical mind is involved instead, what arrives is filtered and doesn't have the same value anymore.

Clairvoyance carries with it a great responsibility, because it allows us to shape the future, the past and other forms of *present*. It is inevitable that the ability to manage the information received also increases together with intuition, because this responsibility "motivates" and gives importance to the intuitive act.

Back to the Chakra model, for enough energy to reach the third eye, the lower Chakras must also align and grow. We must begin to rebalance the relationship with the material world, with our emotions, with the ego and the heart.

This responsibility is therefore counterbalanced by an evolution that every person must experience before having access to this power.

If you want to become a black belt in Karate, you have to follow a master, listen to them for a long time, put their teachings into practice and understand when it is really necessary to start fighting and when, instead, you just need to parry the hit and defeat your opponent by using their own strength.

A black belt in Karate only fights when it is absolutely necessary, because they know how effective their hits may be.»

Real power leads to greater wisdom, because a significant personal evolution is needed in order to manage the responsibility of power.

«So, you are saying that intuition is directly linked to energetic evolution? You were talking about the Chakra model and how to "raise" our energy... is there a connection between these two things?»

«Vital energy and consciousness must raise in order for intuition to become clear, a person must have reached a certain stage of evolution.

Everyone lives some moments of amplified perception, but in order to stabilize this ability you need to work on it constantly. As I said, also working on judgment, awareness, inner calm and personal energy.

In the words of psychologist Maslow, basic needs must have been met and we must be on the road to self-fulfillment. If a person lacks basic needs or lives in the spasmodic search for other people's acceptance, they will find it difficult to deal with the higher levels of their existence, with the higher needs of their being (such as spirituality).

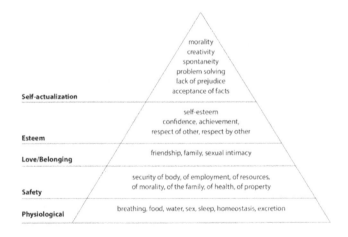

Vital energy, that is, the vital state, must be increased for intuition to happen. It is a journey that takes time;

months or years. We must learn to be *truly present* (like when we were kids!).»

«SOMEHOW INTUITION IS RELATED TO SPIRITUALITY? SPIRITUALITY IS A PREREQUISITE FOR INTUITION?»

«When we talk about spirituality, we basically talk about our relationship with other people and with the universe in which we live. Aside from a religious attitude (i.e. a spirituality conditioned by rules and a belief system), we must recognize the need to transcend our being and overcome our individuality.

When I talk about spirituality, I am referring to a profound relationship, almost an identification with the whole. I am talking about the capability of transcending space and time. This is a condition in which the distance between "I" and "you", between the masculine and the feminine, between giving and receiving, between yesterday, today and tomorrow, is greatly shortened, until it dissolves.

The third eye is a step below the fusion with the whole, it is the point where the opposite poles meet; this is where intuition happens. It is another fascinating way to describe how it becomes possible to transcend space-time, by overcoming the illusion of separation.

Quantum physics describes "quantum entanglement" (you can find a video about it in the *Intuition Training Arena*) as the process that happens when two or more particles relate in such a way that they can no longer be considered independently, but only as a "quantum system". From the moment this relationship is created, these particles react to each other's stimulation, even if they are taken far away from each other. What is more, they do so "instantaneously", exceeding the speed of light. This experiment demonstrated a form of communication that transcends space and time between previously connected particles.

From a macroscopic point of view, we can say that when there's intimacy between two subjects, their bond allows them to communicate, overcoming the boundaries of visible reality.

This happens when we raise our conscience to a higher level than the physical one, where different rules apply.

We have talked about time flow. Time is apparently one of the laws that controls physical reality, but these laws affect your reality in a different way, once you go beyond a certain state of consciousness.»

«HOW CAN A PERSON WHO "FEELS NOTHING" BEGIN THEIR JOURNEY OF DISCOVERING INTUITION?»

«If you don't feel anything, you need to work on your vital state through meditation even more.

Let me explain, if the vital state is below a certain threshold, that sensitivity is so low that your rational mind tends to have the upper hand. Obtuse skepticism is also a sign that a better mind-body alignment can be achieved.

Honestly, I don't think that anyone can "*feel nothing*", but it's possible they don't pay enough attention to what they feel.

I have already described this process. There are two different stages; on the one hand we must learn to recognize information that is already within us and comes to our mind (distinguishing it from thoughts), on the other hand we must prepare the way for this ability as it could be dormant for many years.

Some intuitive information is already reaching you, but you may have been misinterpreting it, you are seeing it as a coincidence or you are giving it a meaning it doesn't have.

Some information may not reach you yet, because you need to prick up your ears a little more and contact that information (and energy) field that surrounds you.»

«SO, PRACTICALLY, WHAT SHOULD YOU DO TO DEVELOP THIS ABILITY? WHAT WOULD BE THE PLAN? WHAT ASPECTS OF LIFE COULD BE MODIFIED?»

«We have already talked about lowering stress and slowing down your pace; meditation in any form, whether you call it autogenic training, prayer, hypnosis... any practice that raises our vital energy can allow us to perceive more.

Practice must be constant, but attention and intention must be even more constant.

Any activity or practice that raises our vital state brings us closer to intuition, be it meditation based on sound (repeating a mantra), breath, movement, mental visualization, hypnotic induction that alters the state of consciousness, guided deep relaxation... but also Laughter Yoga or trance dance increase our energy.»

Chapter 10

«HOW CAN YOU INTEGRATE INTUITION IN DAILY LIFE?»

«You need to bring awareness practices and your inner rhythm to the *outside* world.

I clearly remember the day when my Roman public transport pass was incorrectly recharged by the employee at the counter (which I mentioned in chapter 6). That morning I woke up, I was going out for a random walk. I had some free time, I chose to dedicate that time to myself, to enjoy the present moment... I was in my own rhythm.

When you practice Reiki or meditation, you usually "close the door" leaving out your life, your habits and all the emotions and stress that are associated with it. Kind of like going to a SPA. You put a timer on, you define a time to focus on yourself in a protected place. The mind no longer needs to take care of the past or the future, it is not emotionally involved by the rest of your life, because it knows everything left outside that door will wait. We seek refuge in that time and in that protected space to practice.

But actually, the most important aspect of a journey of personal awareness and growth is the integration with the rest of our existence, with all that is around us, with other people, with our job and the systems we live in.

Every day I make sure to bring my inner world out. And so should you.

It's an extraordinary choice; expanding your being to include everything else rather than being swallowed up by the world around you.

As the vital state increases, this becomes easier and easier.

When the right energy emerges, like a wave on the horizon, the surfer must ride it and use it to fulfill their experience of life.

When we learn to be present to ourselves every day, aware of the simplest gestures, we begin to notice new possibilities and new intuitive thoughts.

What does it mean to be in the present, exactly?

Becoming aware of our feet stepping on the ground as we walk towards the office door, being fully present while writing an email or talking on the phone, observing the people we are talking to, opening our conscience to the sensory stimuli of our environment, and at the same time, taking into account our feelings, our emotions, our thoughts...

Doodling with the pen during a phone call, being lost in thought while your ears listen to your friend tell their stories or thinking about bills while you take a walk (or worse, make Love!) with your partner are examples of what happens when we are *not* present to ourselves. It means creating distance between what we live inside and what we are doing outside.

When I talk to a person and my mind is just waiting to answer, actually I am no longer listening, because I am focused on a different time than the present.

When I'm waiting to board at the airport and I am anxious to get to my seat on the plane, I am losing precious moments of life. Those instants may seem insignificant or boring, but that would not be so if we were really *present*.

Instead, "I have to learn to become what I am doing". While I eat, I stay in touch with the movement of the fork moving closer to my mouth. While I chew, I commit myself to live the sensation of food in contact with my taste buds. While I wash the dishes (a highly meditative practice!) I perceive my hands moving over the ceramic…

When I am in the *Here and Now* there is no past nor future, and in this dimension I can access different planes of reality and intuition *vertically*.»

«Easier said than done! But think about a mom waking up at 6:30 am with her little son already crying... She has to prepare breakfast for the whole family, drive her elder son to school and then go to work... How can you explain the importance of being in the *Here and Now* to her?»

«Living the Here and Now is the alchemical process par excellence, the way to turn lead into gold, survival into enthusiasm (from the Greek *Enthousiasmòs*, be *inspired and enlightened*), habits into real life.

Whatever that mother has to do, she can do it thinking about when she will have completed her duties or she can stay in the *Here and Now*.

Actually, you don't need to change your actions, you need to change the way your actions are performed.

I can aim to cook a good lunch and buy the ingredients, enjoying the journey to the supermarket, staying in the *Here and Now*, or I can think about what happens *later*, letting my mind generate anxiety or expectations.

It isn't *what* we do, but *how* we do it that can change our consciousness and bring us to the present moment.

A few weeks ago, on a Saturday morning, I had a couple of hours available to clean my house, do some shopping, prepare some appetizers for my friends and get dressed for their arrival. I felt I didn't have much time and I was racking my brains on the best "roadmap" to do everything on time.

Running around, I finished everything perfectly on time. When I saw the tidy house and the full pantry, I finally breathed a sigh of relief. In that moment, checking my clock, my thought was, "I finished on time, but I wasted the last few hours entirely, I didn't enjoy my actions at all".

Usually, most of our life happens with no awareness (therefore with no pleasure!), while our attention is focused on what happens *next.*

We need to have goals to keep moving, but we also need to learn how to enjoy the ride, take pleasure and fulfillment in every action we take towards our destination.

«WHAT IMPACT WOULD THE EXPERIENCE OF LIVING IN THE PRESENT AND ACCESSING INTUITION BY CHANGING HER WAY OF DOING THINGS HAVE ON THIS MOTHER?»

In the worst-case scenario, she will realize that many of the things she does (and especially many of the negative emotions she experiences) are not really necessary. She will become aware that there is a much simpler (and more pleasant) way of life.

If she insists on living in the present moment, she will easily notice some aspects of her daily life that need to be changed and will find the courage to do so.

Each choice will become more natural and each route will require much less effort.

When I am at a crossroads, my mind may feel confused, seek a logical solution to the dilemma or feel hurt because of the roads it must renounce.

By training intuition and letting life flow naturally, choices will be simpler and wiser.

If you leave your home ten minutes later, you may find less traffic, have breakfast outside once in a while, a mother may be relieved of a burden and children may be enriched with emotions and experiences.

By following intuition, life rediscovers its natural harmony and flow.

If I'm at the restaurant and I'm about to order a dish (maybe a delicious lasagna that I like so much) thanks to intuition, I can realize that maybe tonight *that* is not the right choice.

My gut says, "Take the lasagna!" and my mind comments, "Yes, mom's lasagna is always yummy!", but somehow, I have the feeling I shouldn't order that dish, that evening, because the cook didn't prepare it properly.

If we trust our sixth sense, *the game* will be easier and this will help us avoid the "traps" of our mind or gut (which responds to the conditioning we received).

The same goes for the fear we live in, irrational by definition, which in many cases prevents us from taking those leaps forward we need most.

By training your intuition, you can perceive the thrill of fear and, at the same time, feel the confidence that everything will be fine.»

Chapter 11

«TALKING ABOUT FEAR... I WOULD SAY THAT RELYING ON INTUITION IS JUST LIKE TAKING A LEAP BEYOND THE FEAR OF THE UNKNOWN, TAKING ON RESPONSIBILITY.

IT LOOKS LIKE YOU COULD GAIN GODLIKE POWERS, TRANSFORM INTO SOMETHING BIGGER.»

«For too long humankind has "delegated" powers that perhaps they should have simply recognized inside themselves to God.

Catholicism has accustomed us to perceiving God as an entity outside us, an energy "above" us, to which we attribute the omniscience and discernment between good and evil.

Perhaps these same abilities are much closer and more intrinsic to us than we believe, we just need to have the courage to accept them and live them.

The resulting power will help us to rebalance any new responsibilities.

«THANK YOU MARCO.»

«Thank you Claudia.»

Non-conclusion (Marco Cattaneo)

I have spent years avoiding the idea of writing a book, because the study of the mind and the human being have taught me that *change is the natural state of things* and personal perception is fallacious. Putting my experience down in black and white seemed too much of a responsibility to me.

Finally, as a first editorial adventure, I decided to write on the subject that, less than any other, lends itself to a single "truth" and could be *crystallized* in a lasting work.

The benefit I have experienced in developing intuition has been too great for me to just talk about it during seminars that I organize for small groups of people. This ability needs to be known and demystified in the eyes of most people.

Until now, we have been talking about intuition as the *ability to perceive beyond the senses*, but at this point I would like to summarize this work in some impartial advice:

Let's learn how to live intuitively, to the fullest.

Using intuition does not only mean *drawing on a wider field of information than the present one*, but also reducing the importance of logic and rationality in life, learning to leave room for inexplicable sensations and making *light-hearted* choices that our mind might consider senseless or crazy.

In these years as an entrepreneur and *kamikaze apprentice* I have learned that the consequences of our most reckless actions are always less catastrophic than we believe and that living inside a safety fence, instead, can be really dangerous!

The strongest emotions we experience are the result of mental processes and conditioning. They lead us, in most cases, far from the *truth*. Intuition is the greatest revenge we can take against our "evolved" rationality.

My intention was never to create a "complete handbook" on intuition, since nothing so great can be contained in the pages of a book. There can be no compendium to interpret intuition, but there can be *this book that you have met,* and that, if you choose to use it as a training tool, will help you develop your personal sensitivity and ask yourself new questions.

Don't try to resist the inevitable confusion that your mind feels after reading this book: this is an important element for the achievement of your freedom of thought.

Just start to notice, day after day, all the changes that will happen in your life; some will be more evident, others subtler. Amazement will fill your days.

If you're not fully convinced yet, just ask yourself one question to guide you for the rest of your life: *Are you really happy?*

If the answer is no, now you know HOW and WHERE to look.

Enjoy your journey!

Don't believe implicitly what I say.
Don't accept any dogma or any book as infallible.
Buddha

Acknowledgements

Marco:

I would like to thank Mercedes Cortegiani, master of meditation, Reiki and wisdom, who accompanied me on my journey to discover intuition for several years and who taught me to seek the most important answers within me;

Claudia for her precious collaboration in all the stages of the project (interview, writing, editing and translating), for her *kindness* as a Reiki and Meditation practitioner and for her immense patience in supporting me;

Holly Renaut for her precious help with editing the English version of this book;

Every single person I meet along my path as a practitioner, teacher, coach and trainer; through you I have the opportunity to get to know myself better, developing strengths and facing my shadow areas.

Claudia:

First of all, I would like to thank Marco for this extraordinary opportunity, for his understanding in answering my questions and for his constant dedication as a teacher of Meditation and Reiki.

Finally, I would like to thank you, the readers, for your trust and for your intuition in reading this book!

We would like to jointly thank the group of *reviewers* who, with patience, have read this book in advance, providing us with valuable feedback to finalize the work. We'd also like to thank Amazon Publishing, which allowed us to publish and share this book, while maintaining decision-making freedom on every single written sentence.

Intuition Training Arena

This book is just one piece of the *puzzle* that will help you develop an extraordinary part of your potential: intuition.

The Intuition Training Arena is the essential addition in order to live your journey to the fullest. It is an online space dedicated to you as the owner of this book. Inside you will find tools and experiences to walk with you in your *time travel.*

In order to access your *Intuition Training Arena,* you will need a password (as specified below), which will unveil content that is constantly updated. In addition to the password, you may be asked to provide proof of purchase of this book.

We suggest you come back and browse the *Intuition Training Arena* every time you think of it; you may find new surprises in line with your journey.

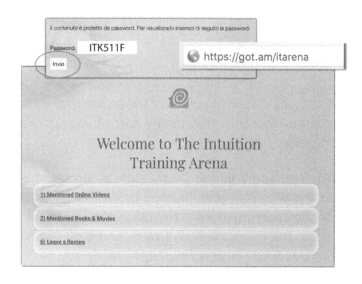

In order to access the guided exercises, courses and free tools designed for you, please visit the *Intuition Training Arena*.

Access to Intuition Training Arena:
https://got.am/itarena

Password: **ITK511F**

Subtle Body and Chakras

The Energetic Anatomy of the Human Being

Marco Cattaneo GOTAM

A New Vision

Life and the entire universe have characteristics that go beyond the sensory perception. Just bear in mind that our five senses are calibrated on specific wave frequencies, and therefore there are sounds and colors that are not perceived by human beings.

Ancient cultures and philosophies have always highlighted the importance of considering situations, as well as living beings, in an integrated way. The contemporary trend is instead to study the single element of each system – as well as each part of the human being – separately from the whole.

We all had the opportunity to experience some peculiar events, strange coincidences that we couldn't understand from a rational perspective. These phenomena are often considered as anomalies of the system, when in fact they are just outside our field of knowledge and, apparently, follow different rules from what we would expect. Everything in the universe is natural: not being able to understand it is not an error of nature, but it represents the limitation of the logical reference model.

Human beings are no exception to this rule. Therefore, the importance and the need to consider them at a holistic (integral, not fragmented) level are becoming more urgent. In addition to the physical body, each of us has non-material manifestations: without necessarily bringing up quantum physics, the fact we are aware of feelings and have thoughts simply highlights how most of our life takes place in immaterial dimensions.

If we want to describe these intangible dimensions (still far from being completely understood in scientific terms), we must accept that every explanation carries with it a certain degree of subjectivity. No perspective – no matter how ancient or traditional – can ever be considered an incontrovertible truth. It must be seen as a simple reference model to understand a new fragment of reality that is still hidden from our consciousness.

When describing the invisible structures of creation, elements such as the chakras and subtle bodies are increasingly being mentioned by many. These concepts should be welcomed as an *evolutionary tool*, to be explored through experience and intuition, rather than seeking to fully understand the subject.

Most of the knowledge contained in this little book is rooted in the esoteric-initiatory, yogic-tantric tradition (dating back in oral form to three thousand years ago and reported in writing in the Tantras after

800 AD). For obvious reasons, these few pages can only convey a simple smattering of the topic, which must be cultivated through a work of research and experimentation, through experience and, as tradition dictates, through moments of dialogue between master and student.

The word "chakra" (Western adaptation of the Sanskrit term transliterated as CAKRA, used in this little book for better readability) means *wheel*. The chakras are vortices located in the energy field of living beings and have the purpose of connecting the adjacent subtle bodies.

The concept of chakra is strictly linked to our personality and way of being: we can consider these energy wheels as some *portals* that filter and bring to our awareness information from less tangible levels of being.

Each chakra encodes data in its own specific light, allowing you to observe any situation from a different perspective each time, like light broken down by a prism showing the seven colors of the iris. Although closely connected to our physical body, the chakras are not immediately perceived through the five senses, since they are located in what we know as "subtle bodies".

The Subtle Bodies

Let's imagine a vase that contains sand, water and oil. Each of these elements will layer sharply over the others, allowing you to observe a heavier band at the bottom, topped by a transparent layer of water and, above it all, floating oil.

Any transformation in one of these levels would affect the entire system. This is exactly how our subtle bodies are structured: defined levels with specific characteristics, yet indivisible and mutually connected at the same time. The vase is the representation of our being in its entirety.

Subtle bodies are as much energy emanations surrounding the person as they are actual *vessels* through which any living being can manifest precise functions.

For example, we can feel emotions because we have the "emotional body" (also called "astral body") and we can express logical and rational thoughts thanks to the structure of the "mental body". Without these *vehicles*, perceptions would be undifferentiated: a kind of primordial soup in which everything is potentially contained, but nothing can really reveal in its individuality.

The physical body is the result of all the characteristics of the subtle energy bodies: what we think and feel emotionally is reflected and manifested on a tangible level.

Traditionally, seven subtle bodies are taken into consideration. However, depending on the method and philosophy of reference, some of these might be classified slightly differently. The seeming inconsistencies are actually useful means to better understand the subject matter. For this reason, it is almost impossible to give an objective and phenomenal representation of a reality that transcends the three dimensions and develops towards gradually less differentiated and more analogical paths.

My suggestion is not to try and find a point of contact between the different traditions at all costs, but to act consistently with the primary chosen model.

Going back to the seven layers, these are as follows (in order from the densest and most material to the most subtle and spiritual):

PHYSICAL BODY: It is the proper body, consisting of the skeletal, muscular, nervous systems, the various organs and apparatuses. It is the result of the characteristics contained in the subtler bodies, to which it is intimately connected.

ETHERIC DOUBLE: The mold that shapes the physical body. As water needs a container to be stored, so the etheric double serves as an "energetic container" for the physical body, being its faithful imprint. Every variation in the etheric double is reflected by a transformation in the physical body. In this dimension, energy failures are manifested in advance, and over time they will turn into physical issues. The density of the etheric double, similar to the physical body, allows us to extend tactile sensitivity a few inches beyond our skin.

ASTRAL BODY: Related to emotions. Thanks to this vehicle, we can experience empathy and other feelings. It is deeply related to the dimensions of sleep and dream, since it is the body that we animate and that acts as a support during the dreaming phase. Also, our awareness most resides in this energy layer during very deep meditations. The astral body is home to the imprint of the emotions we experience most often and most intensely in life.

MENTAL BODY: The first dimension in which the mind, and especially rational thinking, reveals. Here our ideas take shape, together with the beliefs and convictions that constitute our perceptual reality and create the world around us.

CAUSAL BODY (OR HIGHER MENTAL BODY): Mostly related to abstract and creative thinking. The causal body contains the memories of different embodiments that every being is called to experience during their evolution.

BUDDHIC BODY: Its name derives from *buddhi*, that is intellect and comprehension in its highest sense. It is the abstract intelligence, the cosmic consciousness, the seat of universal memory (i.e. the record of everything that has happened and will happen in the entire universe).

ATMIC BODY: Vessel of the spiritual spark, it is the vital flame, something that existed before any common concepts of space and time. It is characterized by a perfect self-awareness and union with the whole.

These bodies are intimately connected, and we can't work on one of them without expecting any changes or consequences on the others. The balance and harmony of the subtle bodies influence the functioning of the physical body, while the energy emanating from the physical body expands like a wave through the subtle bodies (where it can thicken and remain as an emotional imprint or thought-form).

As I've said before, this scheme is only one of the many possible classifications and interpretations. The rational mind needs reference models so it can work on tangible concepts. This is one of those models, but it should not be taken as an unquestionable reality.

Chakras (and we will talk about them in detail shortly) are structures belonging to these energy vehicles, and each subtle body technically has a specific set of chakras.

Thanks to these vortices, information can move from one body to another: the function of the chakras is therefore to connect different energy layers and dimensions, and to transfer energy from the inside to the outside and vice versa.

A visual representation of subtle bodies, much more realistic than some others (frequently used) in which the bodies appear clearly separated from each other.

The Nadis: Energy Channels

The subtle bodies are crossed by several energy channels, which are the etheric counterparts of veins, arteries, nerves and lymph vessels. Each intersection of at least two of these subtle vessels produces a vortex (i.e. a chakra). As the number of intersecting lines of force increases, the amplitude and function of the chakra itself will also grow. You can easily imagine that we have several thousand minor chakras within the body.

Tradition states that the seven main chakras are located at the overlapping of twenty-one nadis, while the secondary chakras are located at the intersection of fourteen energy channels.

The term "nadi" means *flow* and refers to the continuous stream of consciousness that takes place through them.

At the base of the spine, we can find the starting point of three energy channels that are fundamental in Tantric tradition: Ida, Pingala and Sushumna.

IDA NADI: It blossoms to the left and is connected to the left nostril. Through it, the feminine aspect of life energy flows and the characteristics of this dimension (such as creativity, acceptance, letting life flow) are manifested.

PINGALA NADI: It blossoms to the right and is connected to the right nostril. Through it, the masculine aspect of life energy flows and the characteristics of this dimension (such as strength, action and control) are manifested.

Ida and Pingala work alternately, developing from the bottom to the top, twisting and changing direction at various points of the body, until they rejoin at the eyebrows. In case of energy imbalance, one of the two might work significantly more than the other.

To understand which of the two nadis is working more at a given time of day, we must pay attention to breathing: if it is mainly through the right nostril, it means that Pingala is more active; if it is mainly through the left nostril, Ida is busier.

As is clear from their very existence, the masculine and feminine energy polarities are equally present in all human beings, whether women or men.

Finally, Sushumna nadi goes up vertically through the center of the spinal cord. It acts as a supporting column around which Ida and Pingala unfold in a serpentine pattern.

Within Sushumna the vital energy flows, which in its primordial, quiescent state is known as Kundalini-

Shakti. This energy is awakened (metaphorically and physically) by the effects of mindfulness and meditation.

You can see a traditional representation of Ida, Pingala and Sushumna within the modern symbol of medicine, known as the "Caduceus of Hermes".

The seven main chakras are located at the points where three nadis overlap.

The Seven Main Chakras

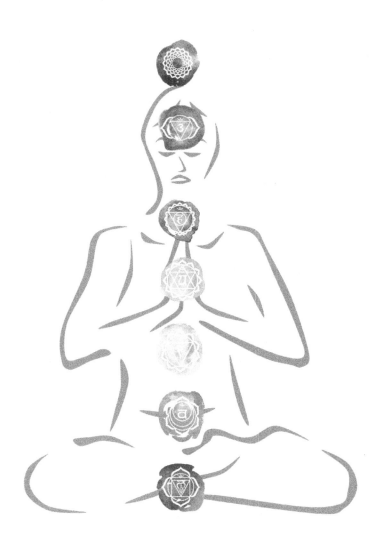

These seven energy centers are located, in order from the first to the seventh:

First Chakra (Muladhara): perianal area, excretory apparatus.

Second Chakra (Svadhisthana): sexual organs, reproductive system.

Third Chakra (Manipura): solar plexus, digestive system.

Fourth Chakra (Anahata): center of sternum, cardiovascular system.

Fifth Chakra (Vishuddi): base of neck, respiratory system.

Sixth Chakra (Ajna): between eyebrows, central nervous system.

Seventh Chakra (Sahasrara): top of the head, peripheral nervous system.

The Structure of the Chakras

Chakras are traditionally represented as lotus flowers, in order to symbolize the ability of human beings to sink their roots into the earth (and mud) and rise to the sky.

As far as the individual experience is concerned, some of them have already blossomed – that is, come to reveal in their full essence – others are still waiting to completely open their petals and therefore require further commitment.

Each chakra has a specific number of petals. These represent the amount of energy flow that branches out from the chakra to spread throughout the body: the energy enters perpendicularly to the center of the chakra, and then it radiates outward.

Each chakra builds some protective structures over time. In children up to about seven years of age, this protective layer (which allows to filter out some of the coarser external events) is still developing, so children are more easily influenced than adults.

Chakras are generally divided into two groups. From the first to the third, they are the so-called "lower chakras", and they are more related to material aspects of existence, personality and interaction with the physical world. They are connected to bodily sensations, well-being, pleasure and survival in a general sense.

The "higher chakras" (from the fifth to the seventh) are connected to the most subtle and valuable aspects of existence, to the relationship with others and with the Universal System in which we live.

The fourth chakra (also called the Heart Chakra) is, at the same time, the dividing line and point of convergence of the two groups. It allows the transformation of earthly energies into spiritual ones and vice versa.

Understanding and using descriptive cards

The following is a description of the characteristics of the seven main chakras. Each one includes an explanation of the specific symbolism, as well as a list of correlations and analogies.

We will see how chakras are associated with a color and a musical note, but there's one important thing to remember. Every living creature has peculiar and unique features. For example, everyone has eyes — but they may be green or brown, big or small. This means every living being has specific colors related to their chakras and these differences will form the features linked to their personality, their behavior and their entire system.

Stating that the first chakra corresponds to the color red and the note C means that these frequencies come directly into vibration with the energy center and re-harmonize it – just like a tuning fork would do with a musical instrument. However, talking about the actual, true color of a specific person's chakra is a completely different story (and, by the way, this cannot be perceived individually as it's part of the multifaceted and dynamic auric field).

In the cards you will also find the traditional mantra for each chakra: the vibration of each syllable helps to nourish and stabilize the related energy center. You can focus your attention on the chakra and repeat the sound several times, remembering that the final "m" (or "ng") should be slightly nasal and pronounced with the mouth closed.

Each chakra is associated with organs, glands and systems of the physical body, which will manifest disharmony in material reality in the form of discomfort and disease.

The evolution of chakras

Chakras exist since birth and we could say that each one is the protagonist of specific stages in life. The first chakra develops in the first seven years, when the child is growing exponentially, both physically and intellectually. It is the time when we learn how to interact with the world, and to live in the material dimension. The next stage is puberty, the sexual maturation that concerns the second chakra.

From the age of fourteen to twenty-one, we experience the formation of our personality, connected to the third chakra.

Next comes the fourth chakra, when love is meant as shared growth.

Twenty-nine to thirty-five years old is the stage of the fifth chakra, which represents the desire to embody our fundamental values in the world and achieve the highest expression of ourselves.

The stage of the sixth chakra opens a window onto an expanded view of the world, where more factors are considered through experience. You learn to see beyond appearance and, in theory, beyond the rough material dimension.

The final stage consists in developing the seventh chakra. It corresponds to the stabilization and maximum openness at a spiritual level, which means finding our own role in the world and within our reference system.

The movement of chakras

Generally speaking, a balanced chakra has a constant and orderly rotational movement clockwise. The first and seventh chakras are represented as cones that connect the human being to the earth and sky (respectively, pointing downward and upward), while the remaining centers (from the second to the sixth) have two cones that share their vertex, developing at the front and at the back.

There are various methods to determine the movement of an energy center, the simplest being the kinesiological test and the pendulum. However, intuitive perception and meditative listening are the most effective ways.

In any case, you can get a fairly accurate idea of the condition of chakras in a person by observing their character traits and any psychophysical problems.

The following pages contain three separate sections:

Harmonious chakra: State of balance and well-being of the chakra.

Deficient chakra: Rotational movement is slowed down; natural energy flow is partially decreased. The greater the disharmony, the more entrenched and severe some of the conditions described will be.

Excess chakra: Hyperactivity of the center, an excess "activation" that results in energy overflowing and difficulty to metabolize it properly.

The characteristics described for each energy condition may occur partially or temporarily.

At the conclusion of each card, I will suggest remedies and strategies to work directly on the chakra in order to restore its natural functions.

Rereading this entire book will be very useful to fully understand the cornerstone concepts of the reality that is invisible to the eyes. Indeed, by the end of the first reading, the seeds for a deeper understanding of these introductory chapters will have been sown.

Muladhara Chakra

The first chakra, which Sanskrit name is "Muladhara" represents the need for stability and concreteness on a material level. It is the energy plexus related to the survival instinct and the continuation of the species and is located in the perianal area, between the anus and genitals.

This vortex points to the earth and energetically connects us to the natural element beneath us, supporting us every step of the way. It represents the need for shelter and food. It is related to excretory functions, hence the ability to let go of what is no longer useful and to eliminate waste.

A balanced chakra provides a sense of security, material well-being, acceptance of the physical counterpart of reality. Its positive characteristics are stability and the ability to succeed at work and financially. A dysfunction of Muladhara will cause problems such as, for example, inability to focus on a topic or project.

This chakra is also involved in our relationship with money, which is considered as a condensed energy form that can be used for material purposes. Muladhara is connected to the concept of greed, not only on a material level but also in feelings and relationships with others.

It is a representation of primordial chaos, a condition of infinite potential and possibility of manifestation.

It sustains our will to live and ensures the vitality of the body.

This energy center controls confidence in ourselves and in life, self-affirmation and also the ability to let go, to change one's way of being and point of view. This chakra typically expresses masculine energy.

| Physical location | Perianal area, between anus and genitals. You can reach the chakra also from the inguinal area |
| Associated physical organ | Excretory system, legs, genitalia (primarily in their reproductive aspect for the preservation of the species), large intestine, blood, teeth, and bones |

Developmental age of reference	0-7 years old (when the physical body takes shape)
Color	Red
Musical note	C
Traditional mantra	Lam / Lang
Natural element	Earth
Harmonious chakra	Feeling of liveliness and physical strength, harmony with nature, personal satisfaction, stability, confidence in life, openness to others, sense of belonging to a group, good relationship with money, satisfaction with what you own and where you live, inclination to work and productivity
Deficient chakra	Feeling that is hard to give and/or receive, underestimation of the material dimension including money, constipation and overweight, tendency to satisfy personal needs while neglecting those of others, inability to adequately nourish the body and to get decent rest, non-harmonious lifestyle, irritation and bad mood that can result in aggression and anger as

	a defense for the lack of self-confidence, fear of losing what feels safe, thoughts and actions obsessively focused on material issues, search for reassurance through food, alcohol, sex and compulsive purchases
Excess chakra	Excessive appetite, obesity, greed, strong yearnings for attachment, carelessness and laziness, excessive pursuit of material stability, recklessness and exaggerated pursuit of short-term gratification
How to rebalance it	Immersion in the contemplation of the red sky at dawn and sunset, outdoor physical activity, contact with animals, plants and earth, barefoot walk, manual labor, massage, Hatha Yoga, listening to the sounds of nature or tribal music. Meditation focusing on the energy center and meditation through the use of its mantra

Svadhisthana Chakra

The second chakra, traditionally known as "Svadhisthana", is linked to creativity, as in the broadest sense of the term. It refers as much to the birth of new life forms as it does to artistic creativity and listening to one's emotions.

Svadhisthana is related to feeling the pleasure and beauty of life, to the experimentation of the world around us through our senses, to the ability to live and integrate our emotions in a balanced way (feeling them fully and letting them go).

Deeply connected to the joie de vivre and sensual desire, Svadhisthana allows us to experience pleasure through our bodies.

The principle of sensory satisfaction that is manifested in this plexus is unrelated to moral and cultural beliefs: the second chakra shows what is a source of well-being and fulfillment for us. Listening to these messages could be a useful way to get to know ourselves more deeply, beyond patterns and preconceptions.

At the same time, the second chakra is where aspects related to guilt and humiliation take shape, it's where the shadow self lies together with those parts that we somehow refuse and to which we deny manifesting. This chakra typically expresses feminine energy.

Physical location	Reproductive system and genitalia. Front: four fingers below the navel; Back: lumbar area, above the tailbone
Associated physical organ	Genital system, ovaries, uterus, testicles, prostate, intestine, intestinal mucous membranes, kidneys, adrenal glands, bladder, spine in the specific lumbar area, lymph, gastric juices, sperm
Developmental age of reference	8-14 years old
Color	Orange

Musical note	D
Traditional mantra	Vam / Vang
Natural element	Water
Harmonious chakra	Pleasure, vital energy that permeates every level of being, freedom to live one's own emotions, spontaneity and simplicity in dealing with others, courtesy, trust, tolerance, expressiveness, free creativity, desire to expand the boundaries of the world, new encounters and trips
Deficient chakra	Lack of certainty and insecurity in the intimate and interpersonal relationship, sexuality experienced with strong feelings of guilt, excessive sexual fantasies followed by self-repression, dependence on sex as the only source of expression, constant search for a sexual relationship to fill the sense of inner emptiness, rigidity in the body and behavior, fear of change

Excess chakra	Tendency to manipulation, unfulfilling sexual hyperactivity and continuous search for new partners, exaggerated emotional instability, loss of energy from sexual excesses
How to rebalance it	Shower, bath, prolonged stay in thermal pools or in the sea, moonlight, musical pieces with natural sounds. This chakra is sensitive to sensual melodies such as traditional belly dancing. Meditation focusing on the energy center and meditation through the use of its mantra

Manipura Chakra

The third chakra, "Manipura", is the chakra of personality, the seat of the masks and roles that we are called to play every day. Personality, indeed, is that mask we wear in order to express ourselves in our relationship with others. A balanced third chakra allows us to recognize our social roles, without forcibly identifying with them.

Manipura is the expression of the ego and is the seat of the individual will, the need to manifest one's desires and the need for self-affirmation, constancy and determination.

Excess causes inability to remain calm, temper tantrums, hyperactivity, stomach disorders of nervous origin. Deficient functioning, on the other hand, causes low energy, shyness, a constant need to turn to stimulants, and dependence on other people's judgment.

Physiological location of this chakra is the solar plexus: centered on the navel, this part of the nervous system radiates into the abdomen as a series of rays that feed the entire system. Just as the sun is at the center of the solar system, so Manipura becomes the center of our personality and social roles.

It is the chakra of logical and rational thinking, of evaluating rather than acting on impulse or emotional transport. This chakra typically expresses masculine energy.

Physical location	Navel area, below the breastbone, in the stomach opening area
Associated physical organ	Pancreas, digestive system, stomach, liver, spleen, gallbladder, small intestine, muscular system, back, immune system, thermoregulation of the body
Developmental age of reference	15-21 years old
Color	Yellow
Musical note	E
Traditional mantra	Ram / Rang
Natural element	Fire
Harmonious chakra	Ability to assert ourselves without intimidating others, expression of our inner strength, determination, perseverance, acceptance of roles in harmony with our own deep essence, balanced self-esteem, ability to transform and "burn" anger
Deficient chakra	Low energy, passivity in living, tendency to manipulate others, dissatisfaction, restlessness, tendency to blame others or fate if expectations are not met,

	unreliability, spasmodic pursuit of success
Excess chakra	Easy to get angry, intolerance, excessively judgmental and demanding personality, arrogance, sense of omnipotence and superiority, intense emotional outbursts, maniacal commitment to work, perfectionism, obstinacy, unbridled ambition
How to rebalance it	Exposure to the sun and to all those natural forms that can represent it (such as sunflower fields or ripe wheat), meditation on the element fire, exercises of controlled breath, cathartic music to release congested emotions. Meditation focused on the chakra and meditation through the use of its mantra

Anahata Chakra

"Anahata" is the great transformer, the balance point between the earth and spiritual chakras. It is located in the center of the chest, at the level of the cardiac organ.

To this plexus is linked the concept of superior love, not to be considered in a selfish or sensual way, but in its unconditional and compassionate form. This involves taking actions aimed at the growth and well-being of the other person, ourselves or the entire system - without expecting anything in return or claiming to decide how the gift should be used by the receiver.

It is also known as the Heart energy center and is connected to the breath and our openness to life. Anahata integrates and balances the body and mind, the individual self in the collective.

Anahata allows us to reach a deep connection with one another, above the aspects inherent to personality and character.

This chakra typically expresses feminine energy.

Physical location	Cardiac region, between the 4th and 5th thoracic vertebrae. Front: heart area; Back: between the shoulder blades
Associated physical organ	Heart, lungs, bronchi, the deepest part of the trachea, arms, hands, upper torso, thymus gland. The chakra controls blood pressure
Developmental age of reference	22-28 years old
Color	Green / Pink
Musical note	F
Traditional mantra	Iam / Iang
Natural element	Air
Harmonious chakra	Joy in giving without expecting anything in return, wisdom and inner strength, self-mastery, desire for peace and harmony,

	capability of being empathetic and compassionate
Deficient chakra	Fear of intimacy and deep relationships, vulnerability to offense, dependence on the love and affection of others, sadness, depression, isolation, desire to give everything but fear of loss, fear of rejection, overly serviceable behavior to feel accepted
Excess chakra	Tendency for strong attachments, obsessiveness, theatricality, weak ego boundaries
How to rebalance it	Contact with nature, walking in meadows and gardens, watching flowers bloom, listening to dulcet and harmonious sounds, classical, sacred and New Age music, opening the chest and breathing expanded, silent compassionate and selfless acts. Meditation on the energy center and meditation through the use of its mantra

Vishuddi Chakra

The name "Vishuddi" indicates the chakra of self-manifestation and communication. Thoughts are like clouds in the sky that are constantly changing. However, when words are spoken, thoughts take shape and concreteness, changing the dimensional plane and beginning to interact with the outside world.

The fifth chakra is the point of connection between the inner and outer universe, the energy center that allows the creative force to manifest in matter. By extension, it is the ability to express ourselves, to communicate who we are freely and without fear, to convey our ideas, to share them as equals with those around us, possibly even declaring discomforts or psychological tensions.

It is the chakra connected with the higher self, the divine spark and spiritual Truth. This chakra typically expresses masculine energy.

Physical location	Laryngeal plexus. Front: on the Adam's apple in men, on the corresponding fold of the neck in women; Back: lower part in the nape of the neck
Associated physical organ	Throat, pharynx, larynx, upper trachea, ears, bronchi, lungs, respiratory system, back of the head, mouth, teeth, lymph glands, thyroid and parathyroid glands
Developmental age of reference	29-35 years old
Color	Blue / indigo
Musical note	G
Traditional mantra	Ham / Hang
Natural element	Sound
Harmonious chakra	Ease in communicating feelings and thoughts freely, inner honesty toward self and others, aptitude for listening, low suggestibility, ability to maintain one's independence and self-determination, full, melodious and persuasive voice

Deficient chakra	Coarse and noisy or cold and formal way of speaking, uninterrupted stream of words to confuse others by masking their weaknesses, lack of flexibility and openness to dialogue, difficulty in making oneself heard
Excess chakra	Arrogance, hypocrisy, falsehood, dogmatism, logorrhoea, tendency to gossip
How to rebalance it	Prolonged observation of the clear sky by lying on the ground and relaxing, immersion in the blue sea or contemplation of the water on the horizon, sacred music with high tones and echoes, attention to inner sounds while keeping your eyes closed. Meditation on the energy center and meditation through the use of its mantra

Ajna Chakra

Commonly known as the third eye – both for its position at the root of the nose, and for the intuitive and extrasensory vision to which it is linked – "Ajna" is the energetic center of awareness and is connected to thought. The sixth chakra allows a broader view of reality, transcending the five senses.

It is the screen on which thoughts, mental images and inner visualizations are projected. Thanks to the Ajna chakra we can make conscious and logical the insights received from the energy plane around us.

The development of this center allows for greater control of higher mental faculties, such as concentration, memory, willpower, creativity and inventiveness.

An imperfect functioning of this chakra can cause, in addition to mental and head disorders, the inability to be open and sensitive to others, as well as intellectual and opinion dullness.

At this center come the nadis Ida and Pingala, vessels of male and female energy, which meet here and merge.

Physical location	Front: space between the eyebrows at the root of the nasal septum; Back: back of the head, on the suture between the occipital bone and parietal bone
Associated physical organ	Pineal gland (epiphysis), cerebral cortex, brain, eyes, skull cap, central nervous system
Developmental age of reference	36-42 years old
Color	Indigo / Purple
Musical note	A
Traditional mantra	Aum / Om
Natural element	Light
Harmonious chakra	Great capacity for visualization and intuition, mind open to mystical truths, clear ideas and plans for one's life, clairvoyance of the everyday in meditation or during sleep, access to all subtle planes of reality, expanded consciousness

Deficient chakra	Rationality and intellect prevailing in every aspect of life, exasperated capacity for analysis, difficulty in seeing reality in a holistic way, arrogance and dogmatism, rejection of spiritual insights, radical adherence to one's own opinions
Excess chakra	Tendency to lose one's mind in the most difficult situations, severe state of mental confusion
How to rebalance it	Immersion in contemplation of the night sky so that the mind opens to the vastness and depth of creation, music for meditation or classical music. Meditation on the energy center and meditation through the use of its mantra

Sahasrara Chakra

The seventh chakra, "Sahasrara," is the energy center connected to spirituality and personal fulfillment. It is located at top of the head and the vortex is directed upward (which is why, in some traditions, it is represented completely outside the body). Sahasrara is connected to the spiritual (Atmic and Buddhic) bodies.

Beyond any cult or religious belief, this chakra allows us to feel spirituality as an inner experience of fusion with the whole universe. The recognition of our role in the universe and the feeling of our earthly mission are connected to this energy center.

The energy of this chakra transcends the male-female separation and is symbolized by the thousand-petaled lotus flower.

The blooming of Sahasrara corresponds to the process of full realization of the human being, the so-called enlightenment: the fusion of individual and universal consciousness. The manifestation of this transcendent dimension of human energy has been represented over the centuries by the halo, painted around the heads of saints and masters, intuitively visible after intense meditative sessions.

Physical location	Head crown. It is fully illuminated in the fundamental moments of birth and death, as well as on the occasion of intense spiritual experiences
Associated physical organ	Hypophysis (or pituitary gland, which regulates the harmonious interaction of all other glands of the endocrine system), eyes, nose, upper airway, forehead, peripheral nervous system
Developmental age of reference	43-49 years old
Color	White / Gold
Musical note	H
Traditional mantra	Ogum satyam om
Natural element	Thought

Harmonious chakra	Identification with every aspect of creation, transcendence of space and time, integration of divine wisdom, insights into the divine origins of creation, sense of wholeness, deep inner peace, oneness with others, open-mindedness, wisdom, reflectivity, awareness, good ability to take in and assimilate information, awareness of the infinite possibilities for self-realization, recognition and acceptance of one's human limits
Deficient chakra	Constant sense of exhaustion, inability to make decisions, excessive pursuit of material well-being, inability to process traumatic experiences, fear of the future and aging, obsessive thoughts of death and illness
Excess chakra	Hyper-rationalization, religious obsession, desire to dominate others, mental confusion, delirium
How to rebalance it	Observation of nature by getting lost in the vastness of creation. Meditation on the energy center and meditation through the use of its mantra, meditation on silence and meditation in general

Elements of Energy Development

After considering the characteristics of each chakra and their connection with the natural elements, sounds, colors and organs of reference, we understand better how the reality around us can react to their energy and, vice versa, how the elements can help the chakras to re-harmonize when necessary.

A mantra can be chanted mentally or aloud to harmonize the energy center. Similarly, Tibetan bells or other traditional instruments can be used in tune with the musical note chosen to experience a real sound massage.

The color of each chakra can be worn in the form of clothing, taken as food, or employed as a colored light directed toward the relevant energy center.

Immersion in the natural element can become a frequent practice and observation of how natural elements react to us can result in a diagnostic signal on the status of our centers.

In any case, using of these tools must be associated with a clear intention and awareness of what we want to achieve.

In addition to the elements naturally present in our world, we can work on the harmony of chakras through a number of different disciplines. Some are more traditional – such as meditation, Hatha Yoga, acupuncture or crystal therapy – some are more recent – such as Reiki, aromatherapy or flower therapy.

The developmental age associated with each chakra represents the period of life when the energy of that center has reached its peak. However, a certain energy center will unveil each year, in a seven-year cycle (therefore, this helps us to understand more theoretically than practically which phase of evolution we are living in).

Energy of the chakras must be considered as a dynamic flow in continuous transformation. Chakras are not switches that can be turned on and off or doors that can be open or closed. They emanate waves that react to every thought, emotion, action and event in our lives.

Everyone's balance changes from day to day and even from one moment to the next. At the same time, their *degree of evolution* tends to be stable and constantly increasing, which is why working on our awareness pays off in the medium and long term.

The Holistic Vision

Chakras and subtle bodies help us to understand the deep interconnection between the parts that make up the human being (body, mind, emotions and spirit) as well as between our inner reality and what's around us. They help us to develop a holistic and integrated vision.

Clinical research speaks of the close relationship between perception of the world, emotions and health of the body through Psychoneuroendocrinoimmunology, even though no other science has been able to capture a systemic relationship so crucial between man and the universe in its entirety.

The understanding of the integrated nature of reality has always been the prerogative of an *intuitive vision*, proper to ancient philosophies and religious traditions. The reason for this is simple: the element that connects the inside to the outside is often invisible to the eye.

The Chinese people used to speak of Chi already thousands of years ago, while in Japan they called it Ki, and in India, Prana. In Europe, Hermes Trismegistus used to talk about

Telesmae and almost at the same time Hippocrates spoke of Vis Medicatrix Naturae, while Paracelso called it Munia. Still, Keplero called it Facultas Furmatrix; Goethe Gestaltung and Galvani simply used to call it Vital Energy. Mesmer spoke of Animal Magnetism, von Reichenbach of Odic Force and, as we approach the modern day, even Einstein, Freud, Jung, Steiner, Reich... have talked about energy as the substance that constitutes life.

Only in recent centuries, science has dealt with the infinitely large and the infinitely small things, going beyond the boundaries of what was obvious to the eyes.

Today we know that everything around us is energy, even thanks to quantum physics, but this element has not yet – inexplicably – become part of our popular culture.

For most people, the term energy associated with human being is reminiscent of hippie culture and seems odd, to say the least.

The same people who communicate every day through their cell phones and watch movies on television, for some strange reason struggle to accept that a magnetic field exists around the human body as well. This is generated by the electrical impulses that pass through the nervous system and by the activity of the heart (it is a phenomenon commonly described in physics by the laws of Faraday, Ampère and Maxwell).

[...]

One of the most authoritative researchers who treats the subject and relates it to disciplines such as Meditation, Reiki, Pranotherapy, Acupuncture, Rolfing, Craniosacral, Reflexology, Shiatsu, Qigong, Traditional Chinese Medicine, is American scientist James L. Oschman Phd.

It is Oschman himself who explains why modern medicine ostracizes the electromagnetic reality of the body in favor of chemical compounds: the 1906 American Pure Food and Drug Act basically made illegal all therapies based on electricity, magnetism and light until 1980 (although their effectiveness was already widely known). This act has historically influenced medical research and the teaching of medicine in university to this day.

(Source – *Meditation: Introduction to Mindfulness Practice and Mindfulness in Everyday Life,* *https://got.am/meditation*)

Beyond the scientific point of view, which is not really the subject of this book, human consciousness can easily recognize the connection between the parts through an innate sensitivity that we can awaken in each of us.

If you have found this book, don't underestimate the signals from your inner compass and remember that hyper-rationality is precisely an indicator of energetic imbalance!

To understand reality as a unique and integrated system means to recognize a connection between our emotional plane and the balance of our body, but also between the deep needs of our soul and the consequences in daily life.

The chakra model explains how every component of the universe – from natural elements to planets, from musical notes to our achievements in life – is closely related to our inner state.

Subtle bodies define the relationship between the several components of a human being, but also the transcendent contact between different individuals. The energy of the spiritual body extends indefinitely, until it loses its consistency and relationship with space and time. Through the spiritual dimension we are all interconnected and can communicate, as well as recognize ourselves as part of one single spirit.

Any change in one element reflects on all the others in the system, although in different ways and at different times. A persistent and repeated emotion can generate biological alterations in the body, our behavior can influence the people around us, a thought can stimulate distant people, an emotion can make us take a decision and change the course of events. Thousands of people, who focused on a purpose and a change in the material world, can achieve it through the intensity of their joint intention.

It is not about unconditionally believing the words of the great masters or this little book. You just need to expand your own consciousness and look at the dynamics that connect everything.

Ultimately, we can only develop a holistic perception of self and the world if we are committed to expanding our awareness and amplifying our personal energy.

Frequently Asked Questions

What is the relationship between chakras and nerve plexuses?

Each chakra is connected to one of the main plexuses of the nervous system.

A nerve plexus is a branching network of grouped and intersected nerves, ready to serve a specific area of the body.

As mentioned above, a chakra is like a vortex that forms at the intersection of energy channels that run through the body. The vertex of each chakra (from the first to the fifth) is located inside the spinal column, where the spinal cord is housed, the primary element of the nervous system; sixth and seventh chakras are located in the braincase, therefore near the brain.

There seems to be a fascinating link between the structure of the nervous system and the chakra energy system.

The origin of the first chakra corresponds to the coccygeal ganglion, the second chakra to the sacral ganglion, the third chakra to the solar plexus, the fourth chakra to the cardiac and pulmonary plexus, the fifth chakra to the pharyngeal plexus, the sixth chakra to the carotid plexus and optic chiasm, the seventh chakra to the cerebral cortex.

This correspondence should not surprise: the subtle bodies are emanations of the physical body, just as the physical body is related to the subtle bodies.

What is the relationship between chakras and endocrine glands?

Each chakra corresponds to a gland of the endocrine system. They usually share proper functioning, imbalance or hyperactivity.

These glands secrete hormones, which are released directly into the bloodstream in order to reach every area of the body and trigger specific physiological reactions. Hormones, in fact, allow the transmission of information and regulate the functioning of the entire body. Likewise, chakras act as a channel of communication between the subtle bodies and the different dimensions of the human being.

The first chakra is linked to the adrenal glands. Their location, as the name anticipates, is above the kidneys. Among others, they secrete steroid hormones that are meant to influence metabolism for muscle mass building and male features. One of these hormones, named cortisol, is meant to regulate stress and thus allow the psychophysical system to adapt to and handle external influences without being overwhelmed. Adrenaline, on the other hand, prepares the body for immediate reactions primarily related to survival.

The second chakra is connected to the gonads. Ovaries and testicles secrete hormones related to desire and sexuality. Estrogen is responsible for secondary sexual characteristics in women and prepares the uterus to receive future life; testosterone maintains male secondary sexual characteristics and is a major stimulator of anger and aggression.

The third chakra is related to the pancreas. Glucagon and insulin are the hormones produced by this organ and manage blood sugar.

The fourth chakra is linked to the thymus. This gland, located behind the sternum, is destined to atrophy during puberty. It is related to the development of T-lymphocytes and aims to contain infections by managing the body's immune response. The link with the heart – and therefore with self-respect – highlights the aspect of self-preservation and explains exhaustively how autoimmune diseases (including allergies) are closely related to problems of self-acceptance.

The fifth chakra is connected to the thyroid. Hormones from this gland regulate the metabolism of all cells in the body, also affecting the production of energy and body heat.

The sixth chakra – or third eye – is connected to the pineal gland. This organ secretes melatonin, which is linked to the regulation of physiological (especially the day/night) cycles and represents our biological clock.

The name pineal gland comes from its shape, similar to a small inverted pine cone. Within this formation is a calcareous fluid (which calcifies in adulthood) containing photosensitive cells similar to those contained in the eyes. Therefore, it looks like this gland is actually capable of sensing specific light frequencies. It is still considered the vestige of a human third dorsal eye.

This gland is naturally active during sleep and in the earliest years of life. In addition, it is widely believed that it can be activated through meditation and focusing on the forehead area. Such activation develops the faculty of intuitive perception, the so-called sixth sense.

(For more in-depth reading on topics related to intuition, you can have a look at my first book: *Intuition, Knowledge and Techniques for the*

Development of Extrasensory Perceptions, https://got.am/intuition)

The seventh chakra corresponds to the pituitary gland, which secretes a large number of peripheral hormones and is connected to all physiological and metabolic processes in the body.

Do chakras really exist?

Many people are doubtful about the actual existence of chakras, because the idea of an energetic dimension of the human being is not deeply-rooted in our culture. This kind of concept-bridge between the physical reality and the spirit is hard to even imagine.

The model of chakras and subtle bodies, however, must be considered as one of the many ways to describe reality.

We can talk about chakras and subtle bodies, just as a mathematician might represent sea currents with equations and show two-dimensional cutaways to highlight waves and their shape. We are referring to traditional models intuitively perceived by extraordinary human beings who have described the shape of the human magnetic field by isolating certain aspects of it.

Will we ever get an unambiguous scientific explanation of the chakras?

Many experiments show particular states of skin electrical conductivity at human energy points and channels. However, it'll be hard to achieve consistency between the various points of view, because it's almost like we are explaining the same topic in different languages.

Why is it so essential to talk about chakras and subtle bodies in the West? Because we have no alternative model to consider reality in its entirety and to recognize the connection between body, mind, spirit and emotions; between our inner space and the external world; between us and the others.

Most ancient cultures of the world have similar expressions to describe the human energetic plane and none of these, by definition, should be considered *real*.

These models are born in an intuitive dimension and they must be approached through an intuitive dimension.

This book doesn't aim to describe reality, but to lay the foundation for you to experience energy.

Only through an inner journey, in fact, can we get a real understanding of the consciousness and energy that inhabits our body. This doesn't require a leap of faith: simply allow yourself to experience the seven energetic dimensions through the practices that are offered in these pages.

Someone told me that one of my chakras is closed and blocked, what can I do?

In the colloquial language, insiders commonly speak of "closed" or "blocked" chakras, but we must remember that these are whirlpools of energy, they're not doors.

By their nature, chakras cannot be closed or blocked. If even just one of the seven main chakras was totally "still", the individual would already be dead. But if you are reading these lines, you are alive and just have more or less harmonious chakras. I am well aware that some insist that it is only a subtlety, a pure distinction of language. However, we know that words generate emotions and often those who receive a "diagnosis" of blocked chakra are deeply concerned about their condition – as if it were an unquestionable verdict. They may feel helpless, when instead they just need to work on their awareness.

Each person has one or more disharmonious chakras: it is part of our nature as earthly and embodied beings. We are not perfect and above all we are required to live an evolutionary path through each incarnation. For this reason, practices and meditations on chakras help us balance every aspect of us. There is no need to worry about imbalanced chakras, as they show precisely the issues related to health, work and relationships that are already evident in everyone's existence. On the other hand, it is very important to understand that we have the power to bring more harmony, satisfaction and serenity back into our lives through conscious work.

Speaking of the balance of chakras, we need to understand that this aspect is constantly influenced by the events and emotions we experience. Although certain early traumas have left an imprint that requires resolution, we will have to devote to energy practice throughout our entire existence. This is because while we seek balance, life affects and alters it. Paying attention to energy balance should be part of our daily routine, just as feeding, washing and sleeping.

How can I work on the balance and harmony of the seven chakras?

The summary table describing each chakra includes tools, which you can find in our universe, to help balance them.

However, meditation is the most powerful practice that can affect the energy of the chakras, which is a form of conscious focusing on single points.

Mind and focus direct energy. Breathing, concentrating and dedicating ourselves to our chakras regularly are the tools that help them heal from ancient wounds as well as daily torments.

What kind of results can I expect from chakra practices?

A conscious effort towards taking care of our energy makes life bloom. I can witness firsthand how fifteen years of meditation on the chakras have radically transformed me, allowing me to live my dream life and to enjoy infinitely greater beauty of the universe around me.

Awareness, however, is not conquered in a day. There are no magic wands that make us change without preserving the balance of our existence. Energetic path is a marathon, not a sprint. All improvements are always and simply in line with our deepest desires and with greater serenity.

Certain advance in our lives could happen in a second, but we often limit the ideal release of wounds and trauma – through our unconscious resistances and the desire to maintain the *status quo*. In most cases, therefore, we won't find ourselves changed in the blink of an eye. In hindsight, we will observe a gradual and constant liberation from our pains – the blooming of our existence.

The thought of dedicating decades to build our happiness may seem disheartening, but it is actually the natural process that every person already experiences.

Slightly altering our daily routine by introducing a new degree of attention to ourselves, devoting fifteen minutes a day to meditation, will have an extraordinary effect on us.

Is it dangerous to work on the chakras and their energy?

The risk is seeing aspects of your life change as they are not in line with your desires or deep needs anymore. You could find yourself in a position to no longer bear certain compromises, cultural impositions and social conventions. You could even start to live according to conscience and following your own inner wisdom.

As soon as we talk about invisible energies and realities, many people lose their clarity and start worrying. As natural and understandable as this is, the practices for balancing the chakras are absolutely safe and cannot lead to any effect that is not exactly what we are looking for.

If a person *does not* really want to be happy, live in harmony and fully realize their human and spiritual potential, then they should not be concerned with their energy balance. If, on the contrary, what they really want is to feel fulfillment – as human beings and as embodied souls – a regular practice on the chakras will be healthy and perfectly in line with their desires.

It may be true, however, that the short-term effects of meditations and exercises to balance the chakras may elicit some of our resistances to change and to let life flow. Some people experience emotionally significant moments or profound self-reflections: how would a dead body feel if the blood suddenly starts flowing again in the veins? Probably uncomfortable or indescribably flushed! In almost all cases, however, the sensations experienced by working on the chakras are more than positive and pleasant. Clarity of mind, deep connection with the universe around and expansion of consciousness are regained. If you were to experience intense moments or disorientation, the need to bring life back to flow within you is probably even greater!

Each practice of mindfulness has an enormous power because the intrinsic strength of every human being is extraordinary. The latter must be respected, gradually known and let free to express itself. For this reason, there is no need to rush or to seek a sudden transformation... because we could actually get it, but maybe we wouldn't like that at all (in contrast to what we believe)!

Luckily, our deep wisdom knows how to recognize a useful path for evolution. If we are willing to listen to it without getting in the way, we could be constantly dedicating to our journey for as long as necessary, without any effort.

Do I have to meditate to balance the chakras?

It is not strictly necessary to meditate in a formal way to balance the energy of the chakras, any form of self-awareness, as well as any *external* tool used regularly, can help similarly.

However, using specific meditation exercises is an extremely precise way to cultivate personal energy balance every day and offers many additional benefits (such as the development of specific mental faculties and the ability to manage emotions).

My unbiased advice is to try meditation to harmonize the chakras and get used to it as to any daily gesture aimed at nourishment and survival. It will be a wonderful adventure. If you like, you can start this journey through the free guided practices that you can download with this book. At the end of these pages, you will find the reference that will be forever at your disposal.

Chakras, Diseases and Health

Since through its functioning, each chakra feeds the energy of certain organs and systems of the body, prolonged imbalances or sudden energy shortages can affect physical health.

The energetic dimension of the human being, indeed, acts as an archive of events, traumas and emotionally significant experiences. The information stored will be used by the body to manage its functioning.

The physical location of each chakra reminds us which organs and systems are directly affected by its malfunction. However, health and well-being are often the consequence of an *overall balance*, while important pathologies represent a global need to restore order in the energy system.

Considering our health holistically means acquiring a new power in regulating our body. First, we must learn to take care of every aspect of our existence and, especially, of our relationship with nature and other people, of the way we feed ourselves, of our emotional and physical needs, as well as any deep desires of our soul and those that concern our personal fulfillment.

While modern medicine is often able to pinpoint *how* a pathology originated in the physical dimension, ancient traditions look at every aspect of the human and spiritual experience to help us understand *why* an imbalance is occurring in the body.

In this broader perspective, diseases or discomforts are not inexplicable anomalies, but a precise response to a deep need – and therefore they have a specific cause.

It is far from rare that a profound unprocessed love disappointment can generate a heart issue, or that an emotional addiction can affect the good functioning of the intestine. The sudden loss of a daughter or a mother can generate breast cancer or a crisis of virility in a man could create prostate problems.

From a holistic perspective, every symptom in the body has a psychosomatic origin.

Developing a holistic view of yourself means taking responsibility for your own personal mind-body-spirit system and considering health in an integrated dimension.

If you want to dive in the root cause of each body dysfunction, a useful resource is The Great Dictionary of Meta-medicine by Claudia Rainville (http://en.metamedecine.com).

Our conscience communicates with us precisely through the emotions, discomforts and diseases we experience. Observing and understanding these messages is essential to really get to know each other and to bring out the submerged part of the iceberg, the needs we deny and the fragments of ourselves that we have hidden in the shadows.

It is key to think that a certain pathology in the body has been probably already there for months or years in the subtle dimension.

Therefore, working on the energetic plane could take a long time in order to see effective results on a physical level. And this is not always possible before the body undergoes irreversible biological damage.

The ideal approach should include both regular practice (once a day or at least twice a week) and a more targeted and intense work, when the physical anomaly occurs. However, we need to consider the different timing of each plane. Indeed, a persistent problem in the energetic dimension can last for years before showing up on a biological level. However, when it reaches the physical body, it has to be viewed and treated in this dimension as well, for a more easy, complete and safe recovery. An energetic work aimed at resolving the conflict shall not be overlooked, but it cannot replace conventional therapies.

Our approach towards chronic discomforts and transient inconveniences in our lives is different. Chronic discomforts are not accurately diagnosed by medical science and just as often, there are no actual therapies that can eradicate the problem, while palliatives are provided to keep the symptoms under control.

You will easily understand when working on your energy can make the most difference: medical science won't have a satisfactory solution, but solving that discomfort will still be important for you.

Working on awareness for healing doesn't just mean to focus on a chakra and nurture its energy. It's also about processing the precious information that are unveiled along the way.

I don't know if human beings will ever be able to have full control on their bodies – for sure, this can't happen without fully understanding the mind, spirit and emotions, the result of a lifelong work on ourselves. What I do know, is that we can be responsible for our health right away, by taking care of ourselves on a deep and *holistic* level. This means solving any problems in the physical body, as well as nurturing and letting personal energetic qualities show in our lives, one day after another.

Meditation on the Chakras

Meditation means accessing an expanded state of consciousness, in which the mind simply experiences the present moment.

Through meditation, we can train ourselves to be witnesses of our existence, that is connected to the sensory reality in which we live, to everything that happens around us and within us, without judging or giving any meaning.

When we manage to quiet the mind (usually overexcited by external stimuli) through meditation, we intuitively begin to feel our consciousness again.

But there is more.

Meditation helps to increase our personal vibration, and therefore to improve the quality of our energy. At the same time, we move to a different plane of reality. In the short term – in a single twenty- or thirty-minute session, for example – this will allow us to think and feel the body in a different way, and probably to pause many problems or discomforts. After a common time of adaptation, however, our energetic and physical condition will go back as before. To get to a stable physical change, an average elevation of our energy and a permanent resolution of certain problems, we'll need to repeat consistently our meditations and accept to look at our shadows, while reintegrating them.

Furthermore, meditation is an extremely intimate, personal and daily activity, which is often confused in the Western world with an opportunity to attend a group, make new friends or spend a weekend in a different setting.

By meditating with your focus on the 7 chakras, we have the opportunity to re-harmonize their energy and, over time, steadily improve their condition.

Here's a dedicated practice that you can repeat daily to begin to experience the energy of the chakras and work toward their growth. Try and follow it without judgment, for a few weeks, and write your thoughts in the meditation journal at the end of the book, taking notes of any significant feeling experienced during the practice.

Chakras and Breath Meditation

PREPARATION:

- Sit in the Yoga "easy pose", sitting cross-legged in a natural way (alternatively, remain comfortably seated on a chair);
- Keep your back naturally straight;
- Bring the tips of your thumb and index finger together, the back of your hands on the knees, and keep the other three fingers open upwards;
- Keep your arms and shoulders relaxed.

EXECUTION:

- Breathe smoothly and naturally, breathe slowly, deeply and consciously (staying in contact with the feeling of the air coming in and out of your body);
- Breathe consciously on the 1st Chakra (perineum region), feeling the air coming in and out of that point towards the ground and visualizing in your mind a white light coming in and out of the body in that same point;
- Breathe consciously on the 2nd Chakra (genital region), feeling the air coming in and out of that point and visualizing in your mind a white light coming in and out of the body in that same point;

- Breathe consciously on the 3rd Chakra (navel), feeling the air coming in and out of that point and visualizing in your mind a white light coming in and out of the body in that same point;
- Breathe consciously on the 4th Chakra (center of the chest), feeling the air coming in and out of that point and visualizing in your mind a white light coming in and out of the body in that same point;
- Breathe consciously on the 5th Chakra (epiglottis), feeling the air coming in and out of that point and visualizing in your mind a white light coming in and out of the body in that same point;
- Breathe consciously on the 6th Chakra (between the eyebrows), feeling the air coming in and out of that point and visualizing in your mind a white light coming in and out of the body in that same point;
- Breathe consciously on the 7th Chakra (above the top of the head), feeling the air coming in and out of that point upwards and visualizing in your mind a white light coming in and out of the body in that same point;
- Breathe consciously on all 7 Chakras simultaneously, visualizing in your mind a white light coming in and out all seven points;
- Breathe at a natural pace and stay focused on how you are feeling in this moment.

Chakra and Dimension of Reality

Through meditation, our state of consciousness changes and the energy of the chakras is re-harmonized, so we literally tune into another dimension of reality.

I like to explain it with the metaphor of a video game: the main character of a graphic adventure evolves and conquers their powers, easily moving to a higher level – where they will encounter a new scenario, new treasures and even new monsters to fight. Only by crossing many levels, they will be able to realize their potential, and they can only move forward.

Similarly, every human being can only continue their own path by going from one level of reality to another. Each step is characterized by new thoughts, new emotions, new *sidekicks* and great wonders. For this to happen, however, there are two key requirements: the desire to play and the energy change. In turn, this can happen through (emotional and physical) suffering or through conscious practice. The latter is dedicated to those who openly choose to know themselves, to explore the depth of their being, to challenge their limits and their fears. And above all, to take action before a problem becomes obvious in the body.

Only few people have the courage to walk this path and to do so with precision, being faithful to what they feel. But the reward for them will be immense.

On this occasion, I chose to write a small booklet – perhaps a little inscrutable – because, most of all, you'll need experience and a true act of awareness to deeply understand some of these concepts. As much as you can read or attend courses, only the inner research and the constant questioning can shed light on such profound areas as consciousness, energy and chakras.

Meditation

An introduction to Self-Awareness and Mindfulness
in Daily Life

Marco Cattaneo GOTAM

I. Meditation and Self-Awareness

In my fifteen years of meditation practice, hypnosis and disciplines that influence the so-called *state of consciousness*, I often said that I would never have the courage to write a book about meditation. It would be such a big responsibility.

Who am I to speak of a discipline that has existed since the dawn of humankind, that for thousands of years has permeated Eastern philosophies, religions and cultures, and that for twenty years has come to the Western world in secular form to transform the health and well-being of *modern society*?

Aware of the great responsibility I would have to bear, I didn't write a book on the subject. Instead, I have dedicated myself to writing a *dense booklet*. This will help you get started immediately in the easiest possible way or, if you are already familiar with the subject, it will explain the basics.

This booklet aims not to cover meditation comprehensively, but to give you simple, direct and practical tools to face everyday life as a fascinating journey of self-awareness.

But what actually is *self-awareness*? We often use this expression incorrectly, but direct experience speaks louder than words.

Imagine you've been raised inside a box, big enough for you to move freely without ever wanting to leave. You've been exploring it for years, getting to know all its walls to perfection, mastering every nook and cranny of it. That box formed your entire universe for a lifetime, its boundaries contained the horizon you could see in every direction. Inside that box you experienced every event, encounter and movement throughout your entire existence. It contained your reality, even though you never realized it was there, all around you.

But at some point, out of a pure *act of awareness*, imagine that you were able to perceive the space outside that box. You had never thought that a world *outside* could even exist (and you certainly had never seen the wonders of that world!).

After experiencing that new dimension, full of new possibilities and emotions to live, you felt the urge to act in order to tear down the walls of your prison. Your horizon had become infinitely wider and this new reality fit you so much better. You had been filled with its grandeur, but this time you were aware that new limits (although invisible to your senses) still exist and you can choose to go beyond them eventually.

Well, your current life is exactly like *that* box: you know it all too well and it contains discomforts and frustrations, joys and sorrows, health and relationship issues of your daily life. You are a part of it as well as everything you can see on the horizon in every direction.

An act of awareness can lead you beyond the boundaries of your current reality and help you overcome any obstacles and limits to your independence, in order to discover a world that is much bigger, full of freedom and joy.

While meditation is the tool that will lead you to go beyond your current boundaries, mindfulness (as it's called in Western psychology) is the attitude that you can use day after day to live your life to the fullest.

If you practice, you will find yourself in a new world. It will contain not only the potential of the previous one, but so much more.

The act of awareness has no limit, but you will have to train your consciousness like a muscle in order to use it. Every transformation of the world around you, every problem solved, must begin with an inner act and then achieved through action. All changes and improvements first happen inside, and only then do they happen outside.

II. Know thyself

A little kitten fell in love with a handsome young man. She had fallen head over heels, so she went to the Goddess Aphrodite and asked for her help. Aphrodite granted her wish and turned the kitten into a beautiful girl. Immediately, the young man fell in love with her. The two of them ended up in the bedroom, and Aphrodite – who was watching from above – wanted to put the girl to test: suddenly, a little mouse appeared. As soon as the girl saw the mouse, she left the young man and chased it.

You can change what you look like and what you do, but not what you really are: you were born free and happy. You already know that, just think about it. How do children behave in the first few months of their lives? They follow their instincts: they eat, sleep, express their emotions. They learn a lot and experience without fear. They are fascinated by everything. They look at the world with wonder, they breathe fully and are constantly in contact with the reality around them through their senses. They live in the Here and Now. They look, listen, touch, taste. They usually smile, unless one of their needs is not met. In this case, they just do what it takes to get it, and once obtained, they go back to smiling as always.

When ancient traditions refer to *knowing ourselves*, they are not talking about a mental understanding of who we are, but a profound self-awareness, felt in the present moment and within the body.

Adults have completely lost contact with their original and authentic nature, they don't even remember it anymore. They no longer feel the part that once was a happy and spontaneously free child. The only thing adults feel is discomfort and incompleteness.

But why?

Newborn babies depend entirely (also biologically) on their parents and seek – more than anything else – connection, love and recognition from them.

They live in the Here and Now, of course. But, they are just at the beginning of their journey as human beings. This will lead them first to trauma and then to its resolution, so that they can fully explore their incarnation.

Through the educational process (which, in every age, transmits specific and different ethics, values and rules), they are taught what is *good* and what is *bad*, what they can do and what they cannot do, what they should show and what they should instead hide about themselves.

Children fragment their own nature, deny parts of the original self, build a personality (i.e. the ego, the mask) and an identity that are very different from what they really and completely are – in this way, they are trying not to lose their parents' love.

They come to know "evil" – because it is taught to them – and they will deny important parts of themselves, while trying not to lose praise from their parents and educators.

In addition, during puberty and adolescence, the process of socialization will further strengthen the personality features that were already outlined.

The distance they will have developed from their inner self is the same distance they will show in their relationships with others. The significant emotional events lived with other people will only confirm the need to keep their mask on.

This is where the discomfort and incompleteness – typical of adulthood – come from: knowing, deep down, that you have lost important parts of yourself and have collected painful experiences in your relationships with others.

Pain often hides behind sadness, sadness behind fear, fear behind anger. And anger, in turn, can hide behind immobility, isolation and anxiety.

And here you have it, the most common emotional problems of our time have emerged from the depths of the personality!

In addition, we can also mention what we call *depression* – from an evolutionary point of view, this is just the impossibility of directly facing inner pain and reacting to it – and *stress* – which is the emotional resistance we exert in response to the pressure we can no longer bear.

As we will further discuss in the next chapter, when these emotional struggles exceed a certain threshold of tolerance, our body falls ill in order to cope *in extremis* with those things we couldn't consciously solve.

Knowing ourselves through full present awareness (mindfulness) is what we can really experience with the act of meditation. We can go back to feeling exactly how that newborn baby feels – happy and free – but with an adult body and mind, and a lot more experience behind us.

III. Body, Mind and Health

Mind, body, emotions and soul are inseparable components in the human being, closely connected to each other and interdependent in their functioning.

Eastern philosophies and ancient cultures have been talking about this for thousands of years, but it was only in 1991 that medical science in the West recognized the close relationship between the first three elements: psyche, body and emotions.

Psychoneuroimmunology[1] is a branch of science that explains how the mind, through imprintings of the past and the resulting interpretation of events, manages the functioning of the immune system – and therefore our ability to stay healthy or fall ill – with the help of neurotransmitters and hormones (molecules that correspond, so to speak, to the emotions we feel).

If an unexpected social situation frightens us (for example because when we were children, we were taught *to be wary of strangers* and we internalized this rule), the release of stress hormones prepares the body to fight this potential enemy, reducing our immune system's ability to cope with viruses, bacteria and other pathogens.

We are well aware that guinea pigs, as well as humans subjected to frequent and prolonged stress, tend to get sick and to deal less effectively with disease of all kinds (even chronic or very serious conditions).

On the contrary, if our mind has been taught to react with curiosity and good humor to new social situations, the body will relax. In addition to making new friends, we will remain healthy supported by a strong immune system.

This is just a general example, but it's easy to understand.

Stress is a physiological condition, programmed into our caveman genes since time immemorial. But since our modern lifestyle means that we are frequently exposed to prolonged stress (if not chronic conditions of acute stress), effective management of our inner life has become an absolute necessity.

In evolutionary terms, when we are able to cope with a challenging emotional condition through self-awareness, the body *doesn't need* to express diseases inherent in that condition. But when emotional stress persists and fails to progress, the body remains the only safety valve.

The soul is not a usual subject of study for scientists, but in a way dealing with emotions already implies an organic consideration of human beings, their needs and desires, their ambitions and their place in a wider universe.

Medical science is increasingly moving towards a holistic consideration of the individual, that also takes into account the environment, relationships and *background* in which a disease develops.

In the most common view of wellness, however, people do not perceive their direct responsibility to take care of themselves and their needs to the full extent – and this is the biggest problem. In fact, no matter how much medicine may evolve, no one will ever be able to replace us in meeting our deepest and most spiritual needs.

Meditation, self-awareness and a mindful lifestyle can save us a lot of physical and emotional pain.

After these short introduction (which I hope will motivate you to practice meditation on a regular basis), let's understand exactly what meditation actually is.

IV. Here and Now

Meditation and mindfulness are basically synonyms. Both terms refer to the state of consciousness we can reach when our mind is in the *Here and Now* and also to the process of achieving that state.

Through meditation we can train ourselves to be *witnesses of our existence*, that is, to be *present* in our sensory reality, connected to everything that happens around us and within us, without judging or giving meanings to anything.

The English word *mindfulness* is the literal translation of *sati*, which means "maintain awareness of reality" in pāli (the language used by Buddha for his teachings) and it was created by an American psychologist who wanted meditation to go mainstream in Western culture without any religious implication in the 1970s.

Practicing meditation and enjoying its benefits don't imply or require any religious beliefs. You don't need to rely on one or more gods who oversee our existence nor turn to particular entities.

Anyone can meditate in order to live the present moment to the fullest, stay healthy and unravel knots that limit their lives, regardless of any institutional or religious structure.

Many people don't feel comfortable believing in God or they're simply not interested in doing so. However, any human being feels and knows that they exist beyond the body, that they are not just *robots* and that they have their own consciousness.

This is already an important element of spirituality, which has nothing to do with our religious context or the creed we have chosen to embrace.

Consciously accepting the existence of a spiritual dimension is necessary to fully enjoy the experience of meditation. At first, everything will be rather mechanical and apparently simple, but we will come into contact with our *essence* eventually and we must be ready to face it.

If you really believe you are simply a *biological machine*, without any *spiritus* (breath of life), meditation probably won't help you that much – or at least I won't be the most befitting teacher.

Once again, you can meditate and live a *mindful* existence without any need to become worshippers or religious people, but it's important to remain open to the perception of your own consciousness to fully experience the *Here and Now*.

If you don't think of yourself as a spiritual person, consider the word *spirituality* as a synonym for "extended environment and social context". To devote yourself to spirituality is to consider yourself to be a part of a larger system, that also includes all other people as well as nature itself.

Beyond all the tangible and concrete benefits that we can obtain from meditative practice (which I will discuss in the next chapter), the expansion of consciousness and the awakening of our *spiritus* can be considered the most important ones.

If you're *lucky* and consistent with your practice, you'll be able to experience the natural connection to the universe around you first-hand – and then you won't need any more explanations.

Through self-awareness, we will carry out a process of reintegration of the lost parts of ourselves, unraveling knots that derive from traumas we experienced. Over the years, this will allow us to dissolve the pain, sadness, fear, anger, immobility, isolation and anxiety that we may have accumulated inside ourselves.

From a practical point of view, during the sessions we can experience actual emotional releases together with crying, laughter or a variety of physical sensations.

During meditations, discomfort, pain or real postural transformations may occur. The body, in fact, stores the emotions deriving from traumatic events of life in our connective and muscular tissue. When these emotions are ready to be released, the body gets rid of them and regains a new, healthier structure.

The very journey of meditation will evolve over the years and decades, allowing important behavioral, perceptive and mental changes. Your evolution will occur simultaneously on all levels and will be reflected in the tangible reality around you.

Through mindfulness, over time, we'll have the chance to perceive the *energy of our consciousness* as a feeling that surrounds and supports our body.

V. Benefits of Meditation

If you are passionate about scientific research, I'd like to tell you that on PubMed (one of the most famous search engines for scientific literature published since 1949), at the time of writing, there are over 4,800 occurrences related to the term "meditation".

There are many monitored studies that have investigated the benefits of meditation and its correlation with health and wellness in human beings.

Several years ago, I collaborated with Dr. Emma Seppälä PhD of the Stanford Center of Compassion and Altruism Research and Education for the Italian translation of her research related to this subject.

After more than a decade of studies, Emma published a summary of the outcomes in the didactic article *10 Science-Based Reasons to Start Meditating Today*.

Here's the infographic to recap:

10 Science-Based Reasons to Start Meditating Today

Meditation was once thought of as an esoteric practice or a hippy-dippy activity. No longer. And scientists are showing that it can have tremendous benefits for your health and happiness! Check it out.

For One, It's Totally HOT!

If...

30 MILLION

Americans have tried meditation or practice regularly and if Oprah, NFL players & even the US Marines are doing it, there must be something to it...

It Boosts Your SOCIAL Life

Thought meditation was lonesome? Think again, son!
Research* Shows MEDITATION:

· **Increases** Social Connection
· **Reduces** Loneliness

It May Just Give You A BADASS BRAIN

Research* Shows MEDITATION:

· **Increases** Cortical Thickness, especially in areas related to introspection and attention

· **Increases** Grey Matter in areas related to memory (hippocampus) and thought (frontal areas)

· **Increases** Brain Volume specifically in areas for emotion regulation, positive emotions & self-control

It Also Increases Your HAPPINESS & HEALTH

Research* Shows MEDITATION:

· **Increases** Positive Emotions
· **Increases** Life Satisfaction
· **Boosts your** Immune Function
· **Decreases** Pain
· **Decreases** Inflammation

IT MAKES YOU SUPER FOCUSED

Research* Shows MEDITATION:

· **Increases** Memory
· **Improves** Attention

Not to mention a GIANT HEART

Research* Shows MEDITATION:

· **Boosts** Social Connection
· **Improves** Empathy & Compassion
· **Generates** Helpfulness
· **Increases** Resilience In Hard Times

And the MORE YOU MEDITATE, the MORE YOU BENEFIT...

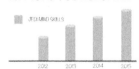

JEDI MIND SKILLS

2012   2013   2014   2015

IT INCREASES WISDOM & GIVES YOU PERSPECTIVE

Ever feel like you're losing sight of the big picture? That you get trapped in the trees and can't see the forest? Try a little meditation to help you take a step back, develop perspective & some keen insight...

Finally, it Beats the Blues!

Research* Shows MEDITATION:

· Decreases Anxiety
· Decreases Stress
· Decreases Depression

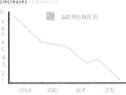

If you are thinking: *"Who the $#@*&! has time to just sit around and do nothing?"*

Then please CONSIDER this:

There Are **1440**

MINUTES IN A DAY...

HOW MANY DO YOU WASTE on Facebook, in front of the TV, or online? That's how many minutes you can devote to meditation ☺

Still don't think you can sit still?

No prob! Go for a walk without your phone or iPod, look at the world around you, be in the present moment, do some yoga or breathing exercises, lay in the grass, stare up at the sky. Take time for yourself. Every minute is a gift. Your body, mind and soul will thank you for it again, and again, and again!

by Emma Seppälä, PhD www.emmaseppala.com
The Science of Health, Happiness & Social Connection
🐦 @emmaseppala
© 2014

As you have read for yourself, there are many measurable benefits that can be obtained through an awareness practice of body, mind, emotions and soul. Meditation really is a holistic discipline!

To sum up, meditation:

- Increases Health
  - Boosts immune system (also in diseases such as H.I.V. and tumors)
  - Decreases pain
  - Decreases tissue inflammation
- Increases Happiness
  - Increases positive emotions
  - Decreases symptoms of depression
  - Decreases anxiety
  - Decreases stress
- Boosts Social Life
  - Increases social connections and emotional intelligence
  - Increases ability to feel compassion
  - Decreases feeling of loneliness
- Increases Self-control
  - Increases ability to handle emotions
  - Increases ability of introspection and self-awareness
- Generates Physical Changes in the Brain
  - Increases gray matter
  - Increases brain volume in areas for emotion regulation and self-control
- Increases Productivity
  - Increases focus and attention

- Increases ability of multitasking (doing several things at once)
  - Increases memory
  - Increases creativity and ability to think out of the box.
- Increases Wisdom
  - Develops perspective
  - Makes you conscious of your creative power and ability to handle your emotions
  - Helps improve talents, let go of emotional blocks and limitations
  - Increases the general quality of life [2]

Do you think that's enough to start today?

Many people come to meditation when they are already overwhelmed by their life – perhaps this is not the best way to begin, but any time is a good time to learn about a journey that can light up your life *for life*. Many others, on the other hand, are already *in control* of their existence and just want to add more awareness and well-being to their daily mix.

VI. Dominance of the Mind

In the most common Western culture and lifestyle we see the absolute dominance of the mind – or rather rationality – at the expense of a bodily and emotional sensitivity that we all need very much.

While the rational-scientific approach allows us an indisputable technological progress and an illusory ability to interpret what we perceive – so that we feel safer – it brings with it an unnatural pace of life and a great deal of stress.

On the other hand, a more sensitive and intuitive perspective can greatly improve our social interactions, let us make *somewhat more magical* decisions and give us unconditional inner joy.

Remember, I'm not suggesting that anyone leaves their work, deprives themselves of all their physical assets and withdraws from the world to meditate full-time in the Himalayas. On the contrary! We were born in a Western country *also* to rely on our brain's resources and evolution. It is inevitable for us to be rational and practical in our lives!

But we should bear in mind that all human beings face critical moments in their lives. In these cases, sometimes rationality can no longer help, so the need arises to rely on the Heart and on a natural transcendent intuition – that is, on the creative mind.

◇

Another potential that most of us underestimate is the body's intelligence.

We are used to thinking of the physical body as a machine that occasionally stops working as it should and *breaks down*, but the most recent scientific knowledge points to a completely different reality. The mind-body system is extraordinarily fascinating and complex, and it reacts to any (internal or external) event by finding a new and more favorable balance. Sometimes, the components of this new balance aren't completely obvious and, above all, there are some unwanted effects evident in the body (i.e. discomfort and illness). But if we acquire a systemic self-awareness (that is, if we are aware of everything that is happening in our system), we would realize that our body is solving a much bigger problem through illness – such as a *suffering of the soul* that we have been carrying with us for too long.

The ability to use our *perceptive* resources must be properly prepared and trained, especially if we are living the classic busy life, with a full-time job and a constant desire to take a break.

For this reason, meditation is crucial.

We must learn to value our sensitivity, at least as much as our mind – which at no stage of the mindfulness process should be set aside or diminished.

One of the clichés to be debunked, in fact, is that the mind must disappear in order to meditate, or that we need to reach inner silence before being fully aware of ourselves.

This is simply not true.

The rational mind – nourished by our memories – performs a task that is essential for our survival: it interprets the stimuli we receive through the five senses and gives them meaning through previous experiences. That is how it creates an *arbitrary inner perception* (i.e. our thoughts and emotions) by drawing on *external reality*.

This is a fundamental function for our lives when we are *not* fully present to ourselves (that is, when we are not meditating) and represents our *autopilot*.

By definition, the mind works by comparing past, present and future with each other, in an *endless inner movement through time*. For this reason, it seems to be keeping us from just being in the Here and Now.

It is not by fighting our rational mind that we will achieve a higher consciousness, but by accepting its helpfulness and using it to our advantage. It makes up and *overcompensates* for the lack of a higher intuitive sensitivity that we had as children and that we've lost growing up.

The trick is to welcome the relentless activity of thought and accept any emotional or kinesthetic reaction to meditation. We don't identify with it and we patiently focus our attention again on the chosen technique.

In a single session, the mind seems to distract us. But in the long term, it provides valuable clues and helps us in our evolution. The mind is on our side, it is a sentry on the alert at our service!

As we redevelop a new sensitivity, the rational mind will get more and more quiet.

Perhaps in a single session, when we are really ready to *feel* our baggage, our mind will surprise us and be completely calm.

As I wrote before:

> *When our rational and intuitive minds work in sync, we automatically enter into meditation,*

in a state where space and time have a completely different taste.

In that state of increased presence, our concerns and the buzz of the world around us just stop. Issues work themselves out (or perhaps we realize those problems never existed in the first place).

When these two dimensions of the mind align and become coherent, intuition arises spontaneously.

[...] [3]

(If you'd like to learn more on the subject, I suggest my first book *Intuition: Knowledge and Techniques to Develop Extrasensory Perception*, https://got.am/intuition)

VII. Give Up Your Expectations

There are countless ways to meditate (I'm referring to traditions, styles and techniques) and unlimited states of consciousness that we can reach – all meditative states, though different from each other.

For this reason, we must try to put aside any expectations.

While we can choose the specific intention of our meditation or focus on practices that can catalyze certain benefits, we can never really *control* the experience of meditation. We can't know, predict or decide what will happen.

The process of evolution through meditation (as a formal practice, that we develop through dedicated sessions) is an extraordinary journey of exploration, discovery, surprise – but often also of frustration, silence, normality and boredom. It's totally part of the game: accept that anything can happen. In this way, whatever may come up, it'll be fine.

In the practice of meditation, it is important to live the experience – whatever it is, no matter how special or normal it may be, however satisfying or not – and not try to achieve any specific goal.

It is the process itself that makes the difference, you are training the *muscle of consciousness*.

In order to obtain the much-praised psycho-physical benefits, keep in mind that you just need some relaxation.
You will find that six slow and deep breaths, with your eyes closed and your attention focused inside of you, will be enough to increase the alpha waves in your brain and relieve stress in your body.

The belief that mental silence is needed to meditate is a misconception.

No doubt you can reach different degrees of *depth* in meditation, as well as there are different benefits and abilities you can develop. But insisting on achieving mental silence is simply pointless.

I am talking above all to beginners (but it can be useful for advanced meditators as well): meditation can also happen *together with the thought*. And the more we try *not to think*, the more we end up generating extra mental noise.

In meditation we cannot consider thought – or any noise in the environment around us – to be a distraction. On the contrary, we should try to include any *potential discomfort* and make it an integral part of meditation.

The more we welcome internal stimuli (thoughts, intuitions, memories, emotions and physical perceptions) and embrace external ones (environmental noises, voices, people passing by, air temperature) the easier meditation will become. Fighting them, on the contrary, will make them stronger!

This information is valuable for *formal practice*, as a lot of unexpected things can happen even if you planned everything meticulously. But this also helps us to understand that we could meditate even *while living our daily life*.

Put aside any ambition to empty your mind or to avoid judgment. Just fully enjoy everything that can happen.

Meditation teaches you to *be satisfied with the journey regardless of the goal you have achieved*.

That is where the great treasure lies: in the present moment, as we take every step. If we don't give up any attempt to reach a goal, our mind won't back down and will continue the useless search.

We can feel peacefulness in the experience, in the journey, for the *duration* of meditation. It happens when we least expect it.

Mindful Breathing

Stop wherever you are.

Shake your body for a moment while you let go of any tensions.

Close your eyes and breathe deeply and slowly through your nose, six times.

Here, you have experienced meditation.

VIII. Where, How and When You Should Meditate

How often do you eat, sleep, wash up? Probably every day, because your body and mind need it to be fit and healthy. Likewise, they need you to take time to meditate on a daily basis.

I will say right away that you don't need to *start meditating every day*. There are many people who have chosen to practice once, twice or three times a week for years, and they have benefited from it anyway.

Many schools of thought, philosophies and disciplines normally impose a daily practice of one hour, some of them even twice a day.

I don't think that meditating for so long is strictly necessary. But, of course, the benefits of meditation are related to the time and energy you dedicate to the practice.

There is no right regularity or standard duration to meditate, because this choice depends on your lifestyle and the result you'd like to achieve.

Unless you are one of those "uncivilized" people who live in full connection with nature, immersed in their primordial rhythm and free from any technological or social metronome – the advice to meditate once a day will always be useful to you.

You can take your time and do this gradually, starting with two or three times a week.

After presenting the different types of meditation, I will give you specific examples of recommended regularity, duration and technique for each person/case.

As with any sport, musical instrument or professional skill, a coach or Master can guide you through your personal journey and help you lay the foundations for your future.

Better to start with a crash course? With a weekend retreat? Or with a normal group session?

My unbiased advice is to start with as little effort as possible, while intensifying your journey over time if you feel the need or if you don't get used to the practice.

A normal individual or group meditation will be more than enough for your first experience.

Should you realize that *you want more* or need an intensive moment to meditate, you can dedicate a special program to it. In any case, just remember that the periodic (and I hope daily) practice is the actual ground of comparison with yourself and your real journey of self-awareness.

No seminar, retreat or single experience can ever replace your dedication in your daily life.

One of the most frequent objections I hear from people who want to approach meditation (and who haven't yet) is that "they don't have time".

I could dismiss this statement by simply saying that we all have the same amount of time and the *priority* we give to our daily activities really matters. Or I could just mention how much time we waste every day on social media or watching TV. Or I could argue with the cliché that *where there's a will there's a way*!

But the unquestionable reality is that the lack of time reveals a lack of willingness to undertake this introspective journey or such high levels of stress that we have almost reached a breaking point.

In both cases, know that you can start meditating even just for five minutes a day. *Schedule this appointment with yourself*, just as you would for any other important task. No excuses this time, *decide today when you want to start!*

For those who want to experience a journey of self-awareness, taking part in a meditation crash course for a weekend or more is certainly not the wisest choice. I myself have hosted these kinds of seminars for over a decade and I would like you to understand that meditation *is not something you learn, it is something you do.*

A journey of self-awareness through psychological disciplines or development of human potential can be explored in depth with a specific course over one or more weekends. But in the case of meditation, you will need to practice regularly and consistently (I hope I'll be able to help you with this task).

As soon as we return to our usual life after any meditation course, the stress hormones will be very efficient in increasing our internal pace and our mind will return to its automatic everyday unawareness. This is why we always need to meditate, especially when we have just started practicing!

IX. Choosing the Right Meditation

Which meditation technique should you choose? Which practice? Free or guided meditation? Mindfulness or hypnotic inductions? Yogic, Taoist, Buddhist...

There can be many questions that nag the mind of a beginner, because there are so many options!

Just as a child who begins to discover sports can experience different activities, you too can play and explore this fascinating universe that will open up to you.

As a general rule, the simpler the technique, the more challenging it will be for a beginner. The more structured the technique, the more easily you will live the experience as you're guided step by step.

Meditation can either involve just the meditator's will power or be supported by a Master's verbal and energetic guidance.

As said before, we don't need to join a specific philosophy or religion in order to meditate.

We can meditate while walking and paying attention to our steps and our feet touching the ground;

We can meditate while breathing at our natural pace, constantly bringing our attention back to our breath should we notice we're being drawn to thoughts;

We can use controlled breathing (like in Prāṇāyāma Yoga) and energize the body by using the empowering effect of breath and ancient Eastern techniques;

We can meditate by moving freely and trying to live the present moment to the fullest through our body (in this sense, Osho's dynamic meditation is quite famous);

We can meditate by flowing in controlled movements through Yoga postures (the so-called asanas, that in Western culture are often mistaken for just some kind of stretching or gymnastics);

We can meditate by repeating a mantra, that is a chanting, like in a beautiful Hinduist prayer (or in the super commercialized TM);

We can meditate by visualizing a landscape or environment that is familiar to us, remembering and re-experiencing an inner journey;

We can meditate by staring at the flame of a candle;

We can meditate by listening to hypnotic words that guide us in a *trance* or an altered state of consciousness through the rhythm of traditional percussion instruments;

We can meditate with some music or in complete silence;

We can meditate in harmony with nature while we are on vacation, moving from one place to another during a work day, or even just closing our eyes and enjoying a recorded practice in our office bathroom during a lunch break.

In short, we are really spoilt for choice. We must remember there is no better, more effective or deeper technique than any other, but simply a practice that resonates more with us at a given moment in life.

For this reason, it is crucial to explore and experience what inspires us the most. And always remember, *meditation is about staying in the Here and Now* as much as possible.

Each style, technique and practice will require specific positions, rituals or accessories. Give yourself the opportunity to discover and experience them without any bias.

I remember my beginning as a meditator. The group used traditional music during the practice and my mind was confused by the *religious rituality* that some of the songs carried with them. The Master who was guiding us (and who had nothing to do with any religious beliefs), came to me and helped me understand what was really important. Beyond form and appearance, it was the sense of sacred that I could feel inside me through that music.

Specific disciplines and schools bring with them beliefs and dogmas that accompany meditation. Your consciousness will need to transcend their limits eventually — as is normal in a genuine spiritual journey.

Just flow and be free in your practice, experiment and let yourself change.

In fifteen years of meditation, I've had the opportunity to practice, learn and teach a lot, from the more psychological and Western approach of Ericksonian Hypnosis to the techniques of Tantra and Hinduism, that came to us through Yoga and Eastern religions.

Whatever your choice may be, no matter where you live, at the end of this book you'll find the opportunity to experience many of these meditations with my personal help.

Inside the *GOTAM Meditation Academy*, that you can easily find online, you will discover different levels of guided practice for each one of the techniques mentioned above, that are suitable both for experts and beginners.

X. Examples of Practical Applications

I don't like standard recipes, because they don't take into account the wonderful universe every human being really is. However, I'd like to provide some examples to help you understand how meditation can be tailored to each person's needs and lifestyle.

To someone with a busy and stressful life (from a physical, emotional or relational point of view) I would suggest a guided relaxation of at least twenty minutes every day, ideally in the evening;

To someone who is particularly anxious, depressed or suffers from panic attacks, I would suggest short ten-minute sessions of free and deep breathing, also repeated two or three times a day at regular intervals;

To someone who feels calm and well-balanced, who seeks greater concentration, clarity of mind, creativity and self-control, I would suggest a sixty-minute session every morning, alternating movement and visualization;

To someone who is alone and struggles to be open with people, I would suggest a series of deep heart meditation of fifteen, thirty or sixty minutes a day, to be repeated for at least three weeks;

To someone with a hectic pace of life, who struggles to find time for themselves between taking kids to school and a business meeting, I would suggest a meditation of only five minutes, to be repeated every time they feel they've hit the wall (and this needs to be just the beginning, because such a high pace of life is a risk for anyone's health!);

To someone who has issues related to physical pleasure and sexuality, I would suggest some simple tantric practices to work on perception: fifteen minutes would be enough to feel more sensitive and sensual;

To someone who is always angry, I would suggest a hypnotic induction of forty minutes, to listen to in the morning at least once a week, in order to teach their unconscious mind to trigger more positive emotions;

To someone who is demanding and eager to expand their consciousness, I would suggest a classic *Om* mantra or some Kriyā Yoga techniques, in thirty-minute sessions, at least three times a week.

Did you get the idea? Meditation is a very versatile tool. And the journey through weeks, months and years will be much more important than a single session. This will evolve with you and allow you to work on the important issues that each time in life brings with it.

Whatever technique you choose, I advise you to always meditate at the same time and in the same place, to get into the habit more easily.

XI. Living Meditation

In the first stage of a journey with meditation, you may tend to practice self-awareness only in formal sessions. Later on, you will also begin to integrate *attention to the present moment* into your daily life.

Following this metaphor, after going to the gym to train your muscle of consciousness, you can enjoy the increased strength, resilience and support that this muscle can offer you in more ordinary tasks.

Formal meditation sessions (i.e. those moments when we practice away from any distraction of the world outside) are essential to train our brain and our consciousness to stay in the *present moment*. The process is greatly simplified by this form of *temporary detachment* from our usual life, in order to focus attention on ourselves. An untrained consciousness struggles a lot to pay attention to itself while also dealing with the reality around it. On the other hand, if it were natural to live and perform our daily tasks while paying attention to our inner world, we would have no need to reach a higher consciousness.

However, it is important to start integrating the meditative state of the practice into our daily life as soon as possible. In this way, we don't risk moving further away from our true self while working or interacting with other people.

Meditation can easily become an escape from reality, rather than a journey of *deeper descent into reality*. This is evident from the fact that joining a religious cult often goes hand in hand with the rejection of physical assets and alienation from emotional and sensual life. It is undoubtedly easier to guide the masses to spiritual evolution by dividing life into compartments and condemning materiality so that all attention is paid to the spirit. Unfortunately, however, this approach is poorly combined with our instincts, that are very difficult to sublimate.

The time has passed for dividing life into compartments, because the instincts that move us require our full attention – and this society would probably encourage them to come out anyway (perhaps explosively).

Chances are that we would end up suffering from a real dissociative schizophrenia if we don't make an effort to integrate our parts. The process of fragmentation to which we are subjected during childhood (and described in the second chapter) is already serious in itself. Meditation must be an instrument for self-awareness and higher consciousness *in support of daily life*, not against it!

For this reason, I strenuously fight the stereotypical image of the spiritual master who withdraws to an ascetic life away from the world: perhaps this represents the last step of a journey that very few of us need to complete. Also, this image is often accompanied by a false attitude of positivity and pietism that belongs more to the ego than to the soul.

Most of us need to go *even deeper* into material reality while dealing with the needs of our soul, rather than *consciously ignoring it*. Through self-awareness we need to accept our shadow aspects that were hidden from our consciousness (i.e. those parts of us that we rejected as children) and become *one* again.

When we feel we can experience our emotional dimension (free to get angry, laugh, cry and be happy), our instinctive dimension (enjoying sensual pleasures), our intellectual intelligence and accept our ego-personality for what it is, only then can we express our mindfulness in everyday life and genuinely live the present moment.

After we get used to assimilating any inconvenience during our meditation sessions, we can begin to pay attention to our self-awareness while also working, talking on the phone, walking down the street or even watching television!

Any gesture, work or task can be carried out with more present awareness.

For instance, we can wash the dishes while paying attention to the feeling of our hands, to what we see, what we hear around us, how we feel. Or we can be mindful while taking a walk, as you will experience in the next exercise.

Even after meditation has become part of everyday life, the formal sessions will remain very important. This practice will be even deeper and lead to higher and more intense states of consciousness and – occasionally – very special ecstatic experiences.

Mindful Walk

While you are walking down the street, at your usual pace, begin to slow down and become aware of your breath.

Imagine that you have a control knob to slow down time. Turn it in your mind, so that everything becomes even slower... not only in the way you move, but also in the things that flow in front of your eyes and through your senses.

Keep slowing down your pace, in order to connect with the present moment.

Slow down more than what you feel is reasonable and observe how people around you move, as they become slower as well. Begin to notice new details in the landscape around you.

Look at a building you see every day and discover new details. Pay attention to what you are experiencing inside of you, to the greater openness you perceive and the sense of well-being that arises, while you continue to focus on your breath.

XII. Respect Meditation

In this chapter I will ask you to trust me and some ideas in particular, which might otherwise seem bizarre.

Meditation requires a lot of respect and a certain degree of attention, because when we use some practices we ask our *inner energy* to start moving.

Actually, I've already talked about this in previous chapters every time I mentioned the word *self-awareness.* But I'd like you to focus on the great power that your conscious intention can trigger inside of you.

For most people the word *energy*, related to the human being, calls hippie culture to mind and sounds strange, to say the least.

The same people who use their mobile phones every day and watch movies on TV – for some unknown reason – find it hard to accept that a magnetic field also exists around the human body. This is generated by electrical impulses passing through the nervous system and by the activity of the cardiac organ (this is a phenomenon commonly described in physics by Faraday, Ampère and Maxwell's laws).

The cultural problem derives from the fact that the human energy field was first mentioned in ancient philosophical traditions (using the term "subtle energy"), while science explained its existence *only* since 1826.

One of the most authoritative scholars who deals with the subject and links it to disciplines such as Meditation, Reiki, Pranotherapy, Acupuncture, Rolfing, Craniosacral, Reflexology, Shiatsu, QiGong, Traditional Chinese Medicine is American scientist James L. Oschman PhD [4].

Oschman explains why *modern medical science* is ostracizing the electromagnetic reality of the body in favor of chemical compounds: the 1906 American *Pure Food and Drug Act* basically classified as illegal all therapies based on electricity, magnetism and light until 1980 (although their effectiveness was already widely known). This act has historically influenced medical research and the teaching of medicine in universities until today.

Every time I talk about energy, I implicitly refer to our consciousness. It doesn't just control the functioning of our body with the exchange of information through its parts, it is also the way we can be connected to all the people around us.

Thanks to meditation, you will directly interact with that energy called consciousness and you'll see amazing changes in your life and the world you live in.

The strength of your consciousness is an essential element in the journey of self-awareness and it will become more and more tangible over time while practicing meditation.

Your increased energy will free an unlimited potential in yourself. That is why – should you feel overwhelmed or unable to manage this power – I invite you to look for someone who can guide you through the next steps of your journey.

For thousands of years, some techniques have been an exclusive prerogative of the elite and were kept secret precisely because of their great power. The indiscriminate spread of information and knowledge that was once only reserved for a few people, gave credit to practices with strongly evolutionary effects, but also very destabilizing for someone who is simply not ready.

As in the learning of any discipline or sport, a Master can help you with their experience and wisdom. However, you will always have to find a balance for your consciousness through a constant and regular practice, for a smooth journey without any speed bumps.

◇

In addition to the power of human energy, ancient traditions commonly refer to the *importance of the Heart* and its *openness*.

Through Oschman's encyclopedic collection of information, we learn that the cardiac organ produces a number of *energy frequencies* that propagate through the circulatory system and reach every cell in the body. The fastest signal is the electromagnetic pulse – that can be measured with electrocardiography and magnetocardiography – followed by the sound wave of the heartbeat, the pressure wave and finally the infrared radiation.

The heart, as a physical organ, represents the most important regulator for the correct functioning of the body (its magnetic field can be detected over four meters away from us!). On the other hand, as an energy center, it represents the gateway to a deep and unconditional relationship with ourselves and with the world around us.

When you choose to use meditation as an instrument of *openness to life*, new information will come to your knowledge and help you pursue this long process.

XIII. Bringing Humanity Together

According to different philosophies and religions, human beings must reunite, as scattered parts of a single being, as separate souls *at birth* who need to return to feeling as *one*.

If we look at the behavior of a child, not yet *spoiled* by personality development, we can understand the distance we have put between us and other people as we were growing up. That child knows how to live happily in close physical and emotional contact with everyone else, without boundaries or distrust, without the need for an armor or any kind of protection. That child doesn't feel separate from other people when touching or communicating with them. That child is much wiser than all of us. But growing up is about structure and moving away from the original one we once were. That *one*, like our personality, split into parts to allow us to live our journey and finally recognize ourselves again in unity.

Senses seem to deceive us, because differences in our personalities make us seem so diverse and distant, but underneath it all we are perfectly the same.

Through the process of raising consciousness you can really touch and feel this affinity and unity in your body and mind, *even just for a moment*.

By meditating, we first recompose our parts, and then reunite into a large global family.

This is not an abstract concept or a belief to be accepted. The illusion of separation that we see in the material dimension is as real as the deep connection that links us all on a higher level. The difference lies in the inner openness and self-awareness that we have to achieve in order to perceive both nuances of reality.

With meditation we can really go beyond the limits of space and time of the rational mind, and access new perceptions about ourselves and the universe through intuition.

If you'd like to experience the wonders of this thousand-year-old practice to which your self-consciousness has already begun to open up, I'll be happy to help you day by day through the *GOTAM Meditation Academy*, which bears my name, and in a way, comprises my legacy. Over the years, the *Academy* has brought together hundreds of meditators from all over Italy and Europe. Through guided practices, courses, and group sessions, you will be able to experience the most practical dimension of meditation (which can hardly be entrusted to the pages of a book).

No matter where you are, technology gives us the unique chance to bring our intentions together for personal and collective well-being.

I can't wait to welcome you with plenty of new experiences right now at

www.got.am/academy

Thank you for reading this far, and thank you for letting me introduce you to a practice that will bring even more beauty to your life.

XIV. For the Modern Men and Women

We really need to slow down.

The faster we go, the more our body experiences stress and falls ill. The faster we go, the more we work on autopilot (and we easily risk going off the road). The faster we go, the more we allow duty to take precedence over pleasure. The faster we go, the more we suffer social conditioning. The faster we go, the more we give up our intuitive and creative power. The faster we go, the more our mistakes are difficult to fix and the farther we find ourselves from our dreams.

It takes courage to slow down.

Slowing down means letting go of tension and healing our mind and body. Slowing down means starting to breathe again at our natural pace. Slowing down means giving ourselves the chance to grasp the beauty of life. Slowing down means noticing new details in every little thing. Slowing down means allowing problems to solve themselves. Slowing down means being able to deeply feel ourselves and other people. Slowing down means being able to choose wisely. Slowing down means knowing how to fix mistakes before it's too late. Slowing down means recognizing the meaning of life.

Slowing down means living in Love.

Extra: Exercises to increase presence of mind

In addition to experiencing meditation through formal sessions in the *Academy*, I encourage you to practice the suggestions in the following pages and bring greater awareness to the simplest actions of your daily life.

Paying attention to the present moment during routine activities is no easy challenge, but it is a powerful tool for the transformation of our awareness and our serenity.

In addition, you will amplify your perceptions and realize how some behaviors may change (or simply take on a new meaning) because you choose to experience them with a different level of awareness.

Repeat each exercise for several consecutive days. This way, you will increase its strength. You can write down your impressions and comments in the blank pages at the end of this book.

Mindful Eating

At a meal eaten alone, begin by preparing the space and making it quiet and without any distractions.

Eat consciously.

Pay attention to every movement as you bring your fork or spoon to your mouth.

Prepare each bite, chew and fully enjoy everything you eat.

Feel any physical perception, in the mouth, down the esophagus, in the stomach....

Remember to feel the fullness that develops within you with each bite.

Listening to the Silence

Rather than spending time looking at your smartphone or watching television, at home or during a quiet moment in your day, choose to stop and simply listen to the silence.

Don't take any action or turn your attention to your thoughts.

Instead, stay physically still, soften your gaze and the muscles around your eyes.

Breathe deeply, three times.

Stay in the perception of silence and enjoy it for a few minutes.

Enhanced Touch

Get some objects of different materials and textures and keep them next to you.

Close your eyes.

Take three long, deep breaths.

Hold one of the objects and feel it through touch, moving your hands slowly over its surface.

Stop any thoughts or judgment, simply connect with each physical perception.

Move on to the next object and continue to feel any sensations.

Deep Relationship

Try this exercise with a friend or family member.

Sit facing each other, keeping your hands close together as comfortably as possible.

Close your eyes.

Take three long, deep breaths together.

Remain in the silent perception of each other.

Grounding 1

Sit with your bare feet firmly on the ground.

Close your eyes.

Take three long, deep breaths. Bring your attention from the feet to the head during inhalation and from the head to the feet during exhalation.

Suspend judgment, simply stay in touch with any physical sensation.

Now focus your attention on the sensation of contact between your feet and the floor, for a few moments.

Then, imagine breathing from the feet, absorbing nourishment from the ground and letting go any tensions of the body *from* the feet *to* the ground.

Grounding 2

Stand upright, keeping your bare feet firmly on the ground and slightly apart.

Bend your knees slightly and close your eyes.

Take three long, deep breaths. Bring your attention from the feet to the head during inhalation and from the head to the feet during exhalation.

Now imagine breathing from the feet, absorbing nourishment from the ground and letting go any tensions of the body *from* the feet *to* the ground.

Suspend judgment, simply stay in touch with any physical sensation.

Breathing in Contact with Nature

Sit in a comfortable position in a natural setting or just looking at a landscape from your window.

Keep your eyes open and begin to breathe deeply.

When you feel calm and fully present, imagine bringing that landscape into yourself each time you inhale and bringing your consciousness *into the landscape* each time you exhale.

Exposure to the Sun

Expose yourself to sunlight.

Sit or lie down in a quiet surrounding.

Begin to breathe slowly and deeply.

Close your eyes.

Stay in the perception of the warmth that the sun brings to your body.

Don't turn your attention to your thoughts, just stay in the present moment and be aware of your breath and the feeling of warmth.

Free Movement

Choose calm mood music.

Stand in the center of a space where you can move freely.

Close your eyes for a few moments as you bring your attention to your breath.

Go deeper into your body with your breath and imagine lowering the volume of your inner voice to zero.

Move your body freely and slowly, guided by the music.

Simply be aware of every inch of your movement.

Watching your Thoughts

Sit in a comfortable position and close your eyes.

Let your thoughts flow freely.

Watch your thoughts as if they were images scrolling on a television screen and realize that *you are not* your thoughts.

Stay in the awareness of the body and thoughts that continue to flow naturally.

Author's Biography

Marco Cattaneo GOTAM, Hypnotist, Master of Meditation and Mindfulness. He has dedicated eighteen years to practices of personal and spiritual development, coming into contact with many disciplines for the well-being of body, mind and spirit.

From 2010 to 2022, he delivered over 160 crash courses, 250 short workshops and helped people in over 5,400 specific sessions.

He founded the *GOTAM Academy* in 2014, through which he reaches over 300 practitioners every day, supporting them in their journey with one-to-one online sessions.

He lives in Canary Islands and works between Spain and Italy.

Web References

Author

https://marcocattaneo.com

Skype: marcoscnask

E-mail: info@got.am

Website

https://got.am

Table of Contents

SUBTLE BODY AND CHAKRAS

MEDITATION

Bibliography

1 *Psychoneuroimmunology,* Robert Ader, David L. Felten, N. Claude Cohen

2 *Benefits of meditation: 10 science-based reasons to start meditating today infographic*, Emma Seppälä PhD, https://emmaseppala.com/10-science-based-reasons-start-meditating-today-infographic/

3 *Intuition: Knowledge and Techniques to Develop Extrasensory Perception*, Marco Cattaneo GOTAM, https://got.am/intuition

4 *Energy Medicine, The Scientific Basis (Second Edition),* James L. Oschman PhD

Made in United States
North Haven, CT
01 April 2023

34869588R00173